PLANT LOVE

PLANT LOVE

The *Scandalous Truth*
About the *Sex Life*
of Plants

MICHAEL ALLABY

filbert *press*

Page 2: "Cupid Inspiring Plants with Love", a plate
from Robert Thornton's *Temple of Flora* (1807)

First published in 2016
by Filbert Press
filbertpress.com

Designed by Michelle Noel
Printed in China

It was Ailsa who persuaded me that I should turn my attention to plants, Anna Mumford, having encouraged me to write two sort-of botanical books for Timber Press, who suggested the idea for this book, and Doreen Montgomery who has been a constant source of encouragement and support. I owe a great debt to all of them.

Introduction

—

This is a book about plant reproduction. That means it's about sex, so be warned. It's very explicit, too – in describing the way plants do it, of course. Most plants lack inhibitions of any kind but there are some exceptions, as you will see. What they do they do right out there in the open. So I begin by questioning whether it's proper to allow young children to witness what goes on in the parks, gardens, and countryside.

I need to ask the question because as my story progresses it will reveal some of the desperate (and often hilarious) measures plants resort to in their efforts to ensure that pollen meets stigma.

Those measures arise from the predicament in which plants find themselves. They're rooted to the spot, as I'm sure you've noticed. Animals have to move around in order to find food, and their travels in search of provisions also provide opportunities for romance. You never know, do you, whom you might meet on the way to the supermarket? Plants live on air, sunshine, and water. Carbon from the air and hydrogen from water are all they need to make sugars by the process of photosynthesis along with a selection of minerals dissolved in water. Their food is all around them, so instead of wandering off in search of it, they obtain their water and dissolved minerals through their roots, which makes it impossible for them to move in any case. So they're stuck, rather literally. And that's why many of them recruit helpers when it comes to mating.

Their need for assistants changes everything. Animals compete for mates; they'll even fight each other for them. Plants compete for assistants, their pollinators, and that means the game plays out differently. Deceit emerges as a key strategy on both sides of the bargain. Pollinators cheat, apparent pollinators steal without pollinating, and plants deceive pollinators into working without reward. There's very little honesty in this remorseless, ceaseless struggle to reproduce.

At this point you may feel I've gone too far. I seem to be attributing intention and deliberate action to plants, which, as everyone knows, are unconscious automata that respond to stimuli in ways that are programmed genetically. They're incapable of making choices. Or are they?

If plants, or any other organisms for that matter, could do nothing but respond to their surroundings in pre-programmed ways they'd soon be extinct, because it's impossible to programme for every eventuality. The world is full of unknowns. Botanists do know, though, that plants are aware of their surroundings and are able to detect changes. If an animal takes a bite of one, or even a wee nibble, the plant is aware of that and responds chemically, often in ways that neighbouring plants also detect, so they're forewarned. If its roots approach the roots of another plant, both plants recognize that and they're also able to distinguish whether they are different species. Their roots may then grow away from each other, but roots also claim blocks of soil and defend them against intruders. In a word, plants know what they're doing. No plant has a brain or nervous system, but chemical signals travel through its tissues and it responds appropriately to its environment. Awareness of the environment and reacting to it appropriately is a definition of intelligent behaviour.

Since plants are intelligent, albeit in ways that are very different from the way we are intelligent, I must take them seriously. Furthermore, in the spirit of the age I feel bound to adopt a position of eco-egalitarianism. By what right or authority do I consider kings and cabbages as anything other than equals in nature, as Lewis Carroll so wisely intuited long ago? With moral equality must come responsibility, however, and my eco-egalitarianism imposes on me a duty to comment critically on the flowerbed immorality we see so publicly displayed.

Read on, dear friends, averting your eyes where you must. And enjoy.

Michael Allaby
Tighnabruaich, Scotland

CHAPTER 1

RED LIGHT DISTRICTS

Peer into the undergrowth and witness the bawdiness of woodland plants, the subtler assignations taking place in hedgerows and the dazzling reproductive antics employed by desert plants.

Woodland
in spring
—

There's a brief time early in the year when the lengthening days bring more intense sunshine. Patches of snow shrink, frozen ground thaws and grows moister. And throughout the broadleaved forests of the temperate world the oak and ash, the birch and beech, the chestnut and horse chestnut, the hazel and hawthorn prepare to unfurl their leaves. During that brief interval, as the leaf buds swell but the trees do not yet shade the ground, a host of small plants emerge above the soil to spread their own leaves and absorb a little of the warm sunshine. Before long – for there is little time before the trees leaf out and shade the ground – the small plants display their flowers.

This is the interlude between dark, bleak winter and gaudy summer when the woodland floor brightens with the colours of the spring flowers. Isolated specks, small groups, and broader carpets of colour catch the eye, diverting the gaze this way and that, from white to yellow to blue to red as each turn along the winding footpath reveals a fresh pattern.

We delight in these spring flowers. Most have been domesticated, the tame descendants of the wild forest plants bred over many generations to give the bigger, brighter, longer-lasting blooms that cheer city gardens and draw families away from the fireside on laughing, health-giving walks in the park. Children chase balls and each other, tail-wagging dogs explore their scent-mapped world, and parents greet passers-by, all out in the fresh-aired Sunday afternoon because of the spring flowers. 'Beautiful,' some say, 'Better than last year, makes you feel summer'll soon be here.'

Have they any idea, these parents, what it is they are seeing and praising? If they knew, would they commend the scene to innocent girls and boys, inviting small children, none considered too young for the experience, to feast their eyes upon it? For what lies before them is nothing more or less than a vast, shameless, flaunting of sexual apparatus, an orgy in which each plant screams silently for attention. 'Me!' each flower cries, 'See me, take me, I'm right here, ready and willing!'

Heaven knows I'm no prude, but I have to wonder. Should such a blatant public exhibition be permitted? If these were young people, after all, they'd most likely end up in court to have their wrists slapped, and quite right too, these same parents would say.

The parents have an excuse, of course, but one that's a deal feebler than you might suppose. 'They're just plants,' they will say, 'not people or even animals. Plants aren't actually *doing* anything, they're not conscious. When all's said and done they're just *things*, inanimate, lacking intelligence or awareness, and so incapable of causing offence. (And you have to admit they're pretty.)'

And that, if I may say so, betrays a serious bias. Obviously, plants are different from animals. A plant doesn't have a nervous system or a brain, but that doesn't mean it isn't responsive to its surroundings and capable of behaving intelligently. The very fact of their spring emergence proves that plants are aware of what's happening around them. They sense change, not with nerves or the kind of senses animals possess, but they sense it nonetheless. They begin to grow because the soil around them is warmer and moister than it was, they produce flowers because the nights are growing shorter, they extend their roots not randomly in every direction but toward sources of moisture and food and away from the roots of other plants, and when they locate food they absorb it. Furthermore, each individual plant is different and its response to a given situation differs very slightly from that of other plants of the same species. Plants are acutely sensitive, especially to variations in the direction and intensity of light and to being touched. It makes sense. Light means food if you're a plant, and touch may mean something's planning to eat you and you'd better do something about it, such as producing a chemical compound that renders all of your tissues indigestible, often poisonous. Plants treat infections in a similar way, circulating substances that inhibit further attack. So the flowers in the park or forest are the visible parts of highly sophisticated organisms that are far from inanimate.

Okay, our Sunday promenading parents may concede, but plants don't move and sex is all about moving, rumpy pumpy. Well, yes and no. Plants do move but most of them do it too slowly for us to be able to watch them. Unlike animals, they don't need to forage for food because the food they need is air and sunlight, which are all about them, and minerals and water in the soil, for which they search with their roots. To see them in motion, you need time-lapse photography that allows you to watch a plant grow towards a resource it needs or away from a competitor.

That said, plants do have a problem when it comes to sex. Being, rather literally, rooted to the ground they can't go leaping around in pursuit of partners. Instead, they must rely on other ways to convey male sperm to female ovaries which, when you come down to it, is what sex is all about. They need help with this, and many exploit animals for the purpose, taking advantage of animal mobility to recruit servants to carry their sperm to an eagerly awaiting female. They spread the net wide, too, including not just bees and butterflies but monkeys, mice, lizards, and even kangaroos and giraffes.

That, of course, is the reason for the bright spring flowers. The advertisement is not for other flowers, nor is it a bribe to persuade the parks department to provide space for them, it's for the pollinators, which in our woodlands, where monkeys, kangaroos and giraffes are hard to find, means flying insects and, to a lesser extent, birds. Europe and North America do have a few other pollinating animals, but not ones that pretty flowers have any hope of impressing. Ingeniously, the flowers appear not only while there is abundant light on the forest floor, but also while there are few low-growing leaves to obstruct the view, so foraging insects, appearing as soon as the sunshine has warmed their muscles enough

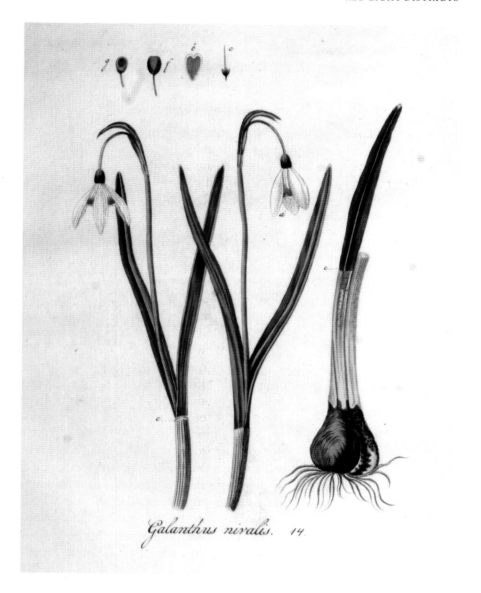

Galanthus nivalis. 14.

Snowdrops (*Galanthus nivalis*) are one of the earliest spring
flowers. Native to southern and eastern Europe, the snowdrop
is naturalized in northern Europe and in parts of North America.

for them to fly, can see them from afar and make a bee-line for the bloom of their choice.

Even then, the wily plants have a few tricks to cover their backs. Imagine you're a plant and, despite your best efforts, no insect calls by? You need a Plan B, and the snowdrop has a knockout one that many other spring plants also use.

From its name you might expect the snowdrop to be one of the first flowers to appear, pushing its nodding white flowers through the last of the snow. When you think about it, though, that doesn't make much sense – and as we've established, plants aren't stupid. If you want to attract insects, why would you raise a white flower above white snow? Part of the answer is that the snowdrop appears after the snow has gone, so its white flowers are clearly visible against the grass or brown earth. The second is that if no pollinating insect arrives, the snowdrop can still reproduce. As the drawing on page 15 shows, snowdrops grow from bulbs, which divide of their own accord, each new bulb giving rise to a new plant. So provided the conditions are favourable, a patch of snowdrops will spread year after year, insects or no insects.

Winter aconite is next in line in the woodland boudoir. A close relative of the buttercup, this little plant scatters splashes of yellow across the forest floor. Yellow stands out against the predominantly green and brown background and is easily distinguished from the white of the remaining snowdrops. The fact that it grows in patches makes it still more eye-catching; the insects can hardly miss it. Its Latin name, *hyemalis*, means 'winter flowering', while the English name of aconite leads some people to believe it's deadly poisonous, like the real aconite, an infusion of which was used to put people to death in ancient times. Winter aconite is quite harmless, however – but don't go round eating it because the early bumblebees emerging hungry from hibernation need its nectar.

The hellebore, another member of the buttercup family, flowers very early in the season with some varieties at their prime in the middle of winter, perhaps in the hope of attracting the first insects of the season. Legend has it that on the first

Christmas there was a young girl who wept because she had no gift for the baby Jesus. Her tears fell on the snow, and where they fell plants grew and flowered. This may be the derivation of the hellebore's common name of Christmas rose. The plant's petals are actually sepals, the leaf-like covers that protect flower buds, and the true petals have transformed themselves into a ring of conical nectaries called honey leaves, like ice cream cones proffered to passing bees. There is another legend in which a hellebore was used as a medicine to cure the daughters of the king of Argos of a madness that had them running naked through the streets, crying out and screaming. If your daughters become afflicted in this way, though, don't make them chomp hellebores or drink a hellebore tisane. These days there are more reliable treatments and you should bear in mind the rumour that Alexander the Great died from hellebore poisoning.

There are two woodland hellebores. Usually the first to appear is the stinking hellebore, which, despite its name, is not particularly pongy, or at least not to people. Insects may be able to smell it because yeasts often colonize its honey leaves, fermenting the nectar and thus raising the temperature and evaporating more of the volatile perfume. Who knows but that the fermentation may also give the nectar a bit of a kick. Maybe the pollinating insects appreciate a warming libation to celebrate the end of winter. The green hellebore flowers a little later, usually from February or March. Parents used to dose their kids with green hellebore to rid them of head lice and intestinal worms. If I were one of those kids I'd run a mile, since hellebores can make you very unpleasantly poorly. The name gives it away. Hellebore is from the Greek words *elein* (poison) and *bora* (food). Even handling them can irritate your skin.

On spring woodland walks you may come across dog's mercury, which has tiny lime-green flowers up to three millimetres (an eighth of an inch) across and is pollinated mainly by the wind, so it's not too bothered about attracting insects. The plant forms green mats that cover large areas,

Dog's mercury (*Mercurialis perennis*) grows wild over most of Europe and the Middle East. It's a member of the spurge family.

spreading by means of underground stems from which new plants arise and shade out rival plants, but not its own kind – dog's mercury grows happily in shade. Its flowers open in February or March to paint the drab ground a bright and cheery colour. It's another one to avoid eating; it's a euphorbia, or spurge, and like all members of that family, it's poisonous. Its common name is a bit odd and may have nothing to do with Mercury in any of its manifestations, as a metal, a planet, or as Mercurius, the Roman name for Hermes, who, among his many other duties, guided travellers, protected sheep from predators, and conducted the dear departed to the underworld. 'Dog' signifies that the plant is of no use – feed it to the dog. Dogs won't eat it, though; they have far too much sense. If you should eat it – but why would you bend down to graze the sward? – you'll regret it, though you'd have to be really ravenous to eat a fatal dose.

Spurge laurel, also called wood laurel and olive spurge, is neither spurge nor laurel. It's an evergreen shrub about a metre and a half (five feet) tall that prefers limestone soils and its strongly perfumed yellow-green flowers open from February to April. The scent attracts bees and is especially important at night, when pollinating moths visit. It's widely cultivated, but beware of handling it because the caustic sap can burn the skin. Native to Europe and parts of North Africa, the plant is very invasive outside its natural range.

As the spring days continue to lengthen into March the woodland floor, especially in the moister and shadier places, turns a vivid yellow as the lesser celandine opens its flowers to the many species of flies that pollinate them. He may have written ecstatically about a host of dancing daffodils, but this was really William Wordsworth's favourite flower. The intention was to carve one on his gravestone, but the sculptor copied the unrelated greater celandine by mistake. Another member of the buttercup family, the lesser celandine has a few tricks that should give pause to those who still believe plants are inanimate. This bureaucratic flower observes office hours, opening around nine and closing at five. And it doesn't like the rain, closing up before the drops start to fall. It aims to attract insects and while it isn't always successful, missing out on pollination doesn't stop it reproducing. If a lesser celandine fails to set fruit it produces tiny bulbils, about the size of wheat grains, and releases them in what country people used to call a rain of wheat. Each bulbil gives rise to a new plant and so, for the lesser celandine, life goes on.

For a while in late spring, yellow is the predominant colour throughout the woodland red light district, not least because that's when lots of buttercup relatives take over, competing for attention with ever-brighter and more abundant blooms. Yellow anemone, also called buttercup anemone, is one of the more spectacular and much favoured by gardeners who plant it in rockeries.

Blues and purples soon follow as the creeping vines of the lesser periwinkle produce their bright flowers, a couple of centimetres (about one inch) across. Violet is the colour bees see best, so in early summer, when the bees are most active, shades between blue and purple scream out for their attention. Lesser periwinkles are often grown as ground-cover plants, but they can be invasive and in parts of North America, where they're sometimes called myrtle or creeping myrtle, they shade out and suppress small tree seedlings. This plant was used in magic in the days when most people believed in the dark arts, and was known as sorcerer's violet. Germans once associated it with immortality and Italians used to place what they called the flower of death on the coffins of dead infants.

Finally, though, the most famous of the spring flowers appear – the oxlips, primroses and narcissus, or wild daffodil. The first is a woodland plant, taller and with bigger flowers than its cousin the cowslip, which is a plant of more open ground. The oxlip stands about thirty centimetres (twelve inches) tall, so its flowers are above the grass and smaller herbs, advertising its delights to bees and butterflies. If that should fail, however, oxlips can pollinate themselves.

More than any other plant, it's the ordinary primrose that draws people to the woodlands in spring. Often it doesn't appear until March, but where winters are mild it sometimes flowers before Christmas. Clumps of yellow primroses, growing close to the ground, brighten the base of hedges, roadside verges, and, indeed, most places that are not too exposed to the wind and rain. You'll stare at a primrose for a long time before you catch a glimpse of the tiny, low-flying flies that pollinate it, as they move quietly and unobtrusively in their pursuit of nectar. The name primrose, or *prima rosa*, means first rose, but it doesn't belong to the rose family, immense though that is. You can eat primroses and infuse them to make a primrose tea, and traditionally the flowers were used to make a country wine, which our grandparents used to drink, responsibly of course. Beware, though, that contact with primroses, and especially with poison primrose (*Primula obconica*) may cause contact dermatitis. And whatever you do, don't mistake primrose leaves for those of the rather similar, and very poisonous, foxglove. Wild daffodils inspired Wordsworth, as they've inspired poets for millennia, their nodding flowers on tall stems blanketing hillsides. It's not poets they're seeking to impress, of course, but the bumblebees that pollinate them. You won't find many insects around cultivated daffodils, though. That's because plant breeders have been pollinating them by hand for many years in order to produce the flower shapes, sizes, and colours gardeners prefer and in doing so they've bred out the features that bumblebees find interesting and attractive.

The plants have three distinct names, daffodil, narcissus, and jonquil. Daffodil and its variant daffadown dilly or daffydown dilly is derived from affodell, a version of asphodel, but the daffodil is not the same plant as the true asphodel – according to Homer, the flower that carpets the fields of the underworld where walk the dead. Narcissus, of course, was the beautiful youth with whom Echo fell hopelessly in love. When he repulsed her she faded away until only her voice remained. Enraged, the gods caused Narcissus to fall in love with his own reflection in a spring. In despair at being unable to reach the young man he saw, he remained transfixed until he pined away and died, when he was turned into a flower. At any rate, that's the official version, and narcissi do grow beside water, their flowers inclined downward as though they were studying their own reflections, but the link is less certain than it seems and the name of the flower may have nothing to do with the myth. The name jonquil refers to the plant's rush-like leaves and is derived from *juncus*, the Latin for rush.

So, as spring draws to a close and the trees open their leaves, shading the woodland floor and declaring the arrival of summer, the parade comes to an end. The orgy is over. Some of the harlots have attained their goal, others have not; either way, the gaudy colours fade until the spring plants have disappeared until next year.

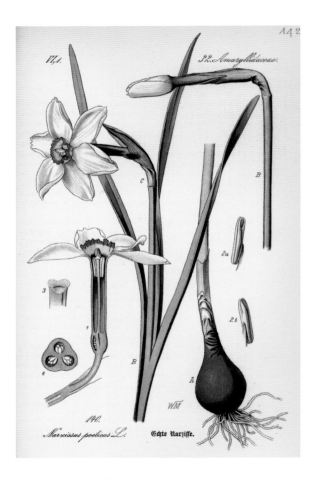

Call it daffodil, narcissus or jonquil, *Narcissus pseudonarcissus*, the national flower of Wales, symbolizes spring.

What is a flower and how does it work?
—

So the spring parade has passed and now the leisured Sunday families must seek other rustic pursuits. But with warm air, plentiful rain, and intermittently bright sunlight, the vegetable sex trade continues to flourish. The trees join in, producing blossom, the hedgerows catch the mood, and before you know it the hawthorn wallpapers the lanes with miles of white or pink may blossom.

But what are they really, these gaily apparelled, often sweetly perfumed delights that appear so suddenly only to vanish a short while later? Well, not to mince words, a flower is the plant's reproductive structure. Its private parts. Its tackle. The flower may be male or female but most flowers shockingly contain both male and female organs. They're hermaphrodites.

Being rooted to the spot, plants search for water and mineral nutrients by growing their roots and they maximize their exposure to sunlight by growing upward and outward, some plants turning their leaves to track the sun across the sky. Where animals walk, swim, or fly in search of the things they need, plants grow in search of them. The form of an animal's body is determined before it's born or hatches, with a heart, lungs or gills, liver, kidneys, a digestive system, and a fixed number of limbs. A plant is less constrained. It has no central organs, no head containing a coordinating brain, a tree can grow limbs, or branches, more or less as it needs them, and in the course of their evolution plants have modified some of their few basic structures, turning them to new uses. All the parts of a flower have evolved from leaves. Petals still look a little like them, but this modification applies to all parts of the flower.

A flower grows at the tip of a stem, called a peduncle, from the receptacle, which is the swollen top of the peduncle and in some species eventually forms part of the fruit. Just above the receptacle there are one or more nectaries – glands that secrete sugary nectar, the food of the gods. If you or I drink nectar we become immortal. (At any rate that's what the ancient Greeks believed. I've not tried it myself.)

The robust, upright central part of the flower in the diagram is the female organ, called the pistil. At its base, immediately above the receptacle, is the carpel, comprising the ovary containing ovules, or eggs, awaiting fertilization. The style extends upward from the ovary and has a swollen top, the stigma, which has a sticky surface.

The tall, willowy filaments around the carpel support the club-shaped anthers and together the filaments and anthers are called the stamens. The anthers produce pollen and the stamens are the male organs. The diagram shows only three but most flowers have many more.

The petals surround and partly enclose the carpel and stamens, the ring of petals forming the corolla. In some flowers the petals are separate and in others they're joined to form a corolla tube. Outside and at the base of the petals are the sepals, forming a ring called the calyx. The calyx protects the reproductive organs and before the flower opens it forms the outer covering of the bud. Together the calyx and corolla comprise the perianth.

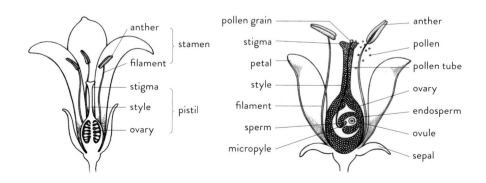

Sepals are usually green, but in some plants they're coloured and difficult to distinguish from the petals. In these cases they're known as tepals.

Below the flower, at the base of the peduncle, some plants have a ring of modified leaves called bracts and in certain plants these are brightly coloured. The bright red 'flowers' of poinsettia are bracts, not petals.

That describes a complete flower, a flower possessing all the parts a flower is able to contain. Not all flowers are complete, however. Incomplete flowers lack some of the parts. They may have no petals or bracts, for example. Or they may be exclusively of one gender, in which case the flower is said to be imperfect, a perfect flower being one with both male and female apparatus. A staminate flower has only stamens and is exclusively male, and a pistillate flower has only a pistil and is female.

When a pollen grain comes to rest on the stigma a pollen tube grows downward from it through the style, into the ovary, and finally penetrates an ovule through a tiny pore called a micropyle. Once the tube has reached its destination two sperm leave the pollen grain and travel down, one to fertilize the ovule, the other to merge with the nucleus of the surrounding tissue, which then develops into the endosperm, rich in starch, and in some plants oils and protein, that nourishes the embryo plant that grows from the fertilized ovule.

LEFT: A flower contains a plant's reproductive organs comprising the stamens (male parts) and a pistil (female parts).
RIGHT: The pollen tube extends from the pollen grain that rests on the stigma down the style into the ovary and enters the ovule through the micropyle. Two sperm travel along the length of the tube and then one fertilizes the ovule and the other fertilizes the endosperm.

That's how it all works, but life isn't simple, we all know that. For a start, only one group of plants bears flowers. Imaginatively enough they're called flowering plants, or angiosperms if you want to sound learned, and they include all the pretty spring flowers, the fruit blossoms, the roses, and the ones florists sell. Coniferous plants such as pine trees, yews, junipers, cedars, cypresses, monkey-puzzles, and all their relatives have a different and more complicated reproductive process based on cones and that doesn't involve flowers at all, though in some species the male cones are coloured and look like flowers. And a whole list of smaller, evolutionarily more ancient plants including the mosses, liverworts, horsetails, ferns, and algae also reproduce without bearing flowers.

So the flowering plants are just one type, albeit a highly successful one. Apart from their dramatic displays, flowers allow for a range of sexual practices that would have made Casanova blush and that has resulted in flowers of all shapes, sizes, and colours plying their disgraceful trade in every corner of the world except for Antarctica, where it's much too cold for such frivolity.

Plants arrange their flowers in many different ways, but the more complex arrangements, called inflorescences and comprising large, often vast, numbers of individual florets, take longer to develop than the single, simple flowers of spring. The plants that bloom in the spring have no time to waste. If they were to take time preparing elaborate inflorescences the trees around them would have fully opened their leaves before the flowers were ready. They would be shaded from above and hidden by the foliage of the shrubs that grow on the forest floor so insects would have trouble finding them.

Asters, daisies and their relatives,
including the dyer's or yellow chamomile
(*Chamaemelum nobile*) shown here have
composite flowers consisting of disc florets
at the centre surrounded by ray florets.

An umbel consists of many florets arranged in a parasol
shape. Very many plants bear inflorescences of this type.
This is the carrot, *Daucus carota*, which is typical.

Spring is all about flaunting it crudely, garishly, and quickly while you have the chance. Refinement is for the more sophisticated courtesans that arrive on the scene later, when days are long, unshaded places can be guaranteed to remain unshaded, and there is time for subtlety.

And with more time to develop their ornamentation, to add embellishments and flourishes, plants are able to produce anything their botanic imagination can conceive. All shapes and sizes means just that. Think of the humble daisy that Saturday gardeners try to chase away with lawnmowers and small children collect to make into chains. Or its bigger cousins the Michaelmas daisy and sunflower, or the aster, or dyer's, or yellow, chamomile. They're all pretty much alike, these daisy-like flowers, and there are well over twenty thousand species of them.

The illustration of the dyer's chamomile on page 27 reveals the secret of all these flowers. What you see isn't a single flower as you might suppose, but a whole mass of tiny flowers, or florets, forming a flower head or capitulum – which is Latin for 'little head'. At the centre there are disc florets, yellow in this example. These are the fertile flowers that produce pollen and ovules – the working flowers, if you like. Surrounding them are the ray florets, each one a very simple flower with up to three strap-shaped petals. 'Aster' is the Greek for 'star' and flowers of this form resemble a bright yellow star surrounded by rays of light.

The ray florets are sterile and serve to direct pollinating insects to the central disc. The daisies, asters, and chamomiles have flowers with both disc and ray florets, but there are others that bear one or the other. Dandelions have only ray florets, for instance, and thistles have only disc florets.

Here's a curious thing. If you count the number of florets in each circle of the disc or the ray florets in each circle of the ray (if there's more than one circle) you'll find that moving outward from the centre the number in each circle is equal to the sum of the numbers in the two preceding circles – 1, 1, 2, 3, 5, 8, 13, 21, 34, 55 and so on. It's called a Fibonacci sequence and it turns up all over the place in nature – and indeed art. The golden section in art is based on the same ratio as the Fibonacci sequence and many a saucy naked goddess has reclined temptingly in what could be regarded as one of the sweet spots of the composition.

Daisies and their chums aren't the only flowers to use outer rings of sterile florets to guide pollinators to the fertile florets at the centre. Lace-cap hydrangeas are built the same way, although the purely ornamental outer florets look like ordinary four-petalled flowers. The lace-cap hydrangea is a type of inflorescence known as a corymb.

Summer hedgerows are crowded with flowers, mostly white or pale pink, of a different form. Summer flowers often consist of small florets arranged in umbrella shapes. Umbrellas are necessary accessories in a British summer so maybe plants also need them, but *umbella* is the Latin for sunshade or parasol and botanists who prefer more southern climes or who sensibly venture along country lanes only on fine days call such inflorescences umbels. The name describes only the arrangement and says nothing about the individual florets, which may be relatively large, like those of the cowslip, or tiny, while the umbel may be anywhere from almost flat-topped to almost spherical. There are hundreds of umbellifers, as they are known. The wild carrot, ancestor of the cultivated carrot, is typical. That one's edible, of course, and so are some of the others, but the hedgerow umbels also include hemlock, recognizable by the red or purple blotches on its thick stem, and the extremely poisonous hemlock water dropwort.

Each floret in an umbel sits atop its own stalk, or pedicel, but umbels can also be compound, the overall umbel composed of many small umbels. Celery and sea samphire bear compound umbels.

Cow parsley is very similar to carrot, but bigger, sometimes as tall as a man. When I was a lad we called all the roadside umbel flowers cow parsley regardless. It made life simple, but was seriously wrongheaded. Giant cow parsley, which can grow to a height of more than five metres (sixteen feet), is also called giant hogweed and contact with it sensitizes the skin to light,

Black mustard (*Brassica nigra*) belongs to the cabbage family
(Brassicaceae). Like those of its relatives, black mustard
flowers form an inflorescence known as a raceme.

31

causing blisters that leave long-lasting scars, while contact with the eyes can cause blindness. It's native to North America and was introduced to Europe in the nineteenth century as a garden ornamental. You do wonder about gardeners sometimes.

You should avoid poisonous plants, obviously, but you shouldn't blame them. Remember, plants move much more slowly than the many animals that would like to eat them and since they can't run away they're entitled to defend themselves any way they can. Some use thorns, some sting, some are very tough or taste horrible, but many use poisons to make certain the would-be diner doesn't return in a hurry. Or at all. There's nothing personal in it. What would you do?

Other plants arrange their flowers differently. You don't often see cabbage flowers because growers harvest the heads before they produce their flowers. But if one escapes the harvester's knife, flowering will make it inedible, so you'll be able to examine the flower, or more correctly the inflorescence. It consists of a central stem, called the rachis, with individual flowers emerging on either side alternately, each with its own pedicel, and the pedicels usually become shorter with increasing height up the rachis. The rachis continues to grow and the youngest flowers are those at the top. This arrangement is called a raceme, and an inflorescence of this type is said to be racemose.

There are several variations on this theme and in due course I dare say we'll meet all of them. The flowers may lack pedicels, for instance, so they sit close against the stem, each with a bract beneath it. The inflorescence is then called a spike and each of its individual flowers is a spikelet. Ryegrasses bear spikes of this type. Others, such as Bermuda grass, have more than one rachis, spreading from a central point like the fingers of a hand, and yet others have multiple spikes arising from different places on the main stem of the plant.

If the spike hangs down it is a catkin, or ament. Hazel, hornbeam, beech, alder, sweet chestnut, and willow are among the plants that produce catkins. The flowers are usually all of the same sex and they're tiny, with inconspicuous petals or no petals at all. You find them mainly on trees or woody shrubs. Hazel catkins are male, and their emergence was traditionally a sign that spring had arrived. Among them, though, if you look carefully you'll find the small, bright red female flowers, waiting for the pollen released by the much more numerous males. The abundance of catkins, and the hazelnuts that the female flowers make with the help of their pollen, varies greatly from year to year, so wild hazel is a somewhat unreliable food source. Nevertheless, the nuts have been an important part of people's diet for many thousands of years.

Alternatively, each branch of the raceme may have branches of its own. Each branch continues to grow throughout the flowering season, producing more and more side shoots, each with its own flower. This arrangement is a panicle. Rice produces panicles of florets, so its grains also hang in panicles, and so do grapes.

If the main stem of a plant ends in a flower, that is a cyme, and in a compound cyme, such as the flower of red campion, the main stem has many side branches, the stem and each side branch ending in a flower. The formation of a flower at the tip of a stem means the stem cannot continue growing, and it is whether or not the stem continues growing or bears a terminal flower that distinguishes racemose from cymose inflorescences.

And all these variations and more exist because over the generations each of them has proved successful at helping the flower to shift its pollen from male to female. Productive sex, after all, is what it's all about.

Flower meadows
in summer
—

The months pass, the trees unfurl their leaves, and the forests become subdued, shady places, with only dappled sunshine reaching the floor, and then only in certain places. It's summer and the traditional time for a very different red light district to open for business. In summer it's the turn of the meadows to erupt in a clamour of sexual display, with flowers of all colours competing for winged clients.

At least, that's the way it used to be. At the outbreak of the Second World War, Britain was importing a large proportion of its food and was critically dependent on those imports. Agriculture was depressed, farmland was sold for knockdown prices, there was little money for investment and, consequently, productivity was low. Then attacks on convoys of ships transporting foodstuffs restricted imports. If the nation was to avoid widespread hunger, possibly starvation, every last corner of land capable of producing food had to be pressed into service. Large areas of previously uncultivated land were ploughed and there were 'pig bins' on urban street corners into which residents were required by law to deposit appropriate food wastes, with helpful instructions on 'what pigs like'. Rationing was strict. But although there was some ploughing up of grasslands, these were less severely affected. Grass was needed to feed livestock, which still included many workhorses. So there were still meadows in the lowlands, permanent pastures that were uncultivated but grazed for part of the year and cut for hay. And, along with a wide variety of grasses, those meadows accommodated countless 'herbs': small plants that throughout the summer raised their stems above the grasses and displayed their flowers. These summer harlots plied their wares.

Did children really did gambol through these flower meadows or is our memory playing tricks? Are we merely projecting ourselves into images gathered from movies and old photographs? Were parts of the countryside really like that? And were summer school holidays really filled with the long, warm sunny days necessary for proper gambolling? Or did we actually spend much more of our time watching the rain trickling down the window while we tried to think of something to do?

It all changed after the war. That was when there was real hunger across Europe and a serious risk of pandemic disease that the weakened population would have found difficult to resist and the medical services would have been stretched to treat. Epidemiologists remembered the flu that followed the First World War, carrying away more victims than the fighting had. So food had to be diverted to the most needy and in Britain some aspects of rationing became even tighter. Now the grasslands had to be made more productive – to be improved – and the way to do that was to plough them up, install drainage, fertilize them, and reseed them with a limited number of fast-growing, nutritious grass species. Grass became a crop. The old permanent lowland pastures vanished and with them went most of the meadow herbs, now reduced to the status of weeds because they contaminated hay and spoiled the newly fashionable silage. Then the Common Agricultural Policy accelerated the process. By 1984 the area of unimproved, lowland, permanent pasture and meadow in England and Wales was only nine per cent of the area that had existed in 1932. The red light district came close to vanishing.

Today we bemoan the loss of all those wild herbs. They've not disappeared entirely, of course, but if you wish to see them you have to know where to look. Flower meadows are likely to have preservation orders on them and gambolling is forbidden. Look but don't touch and, above all, don't tread on the plants.

In these days of conservationist concern we might feel shock at the casual manner in which the adults of those early times allowed their offspring unrestricted access to all this

Yellow rattle (*Rhinanthus minor*), named for the colour of its flowers and its seeds that rattle inside the fruit capsules shown here, is a parasite of other plants. Its presence in a meadow improves biodiversity by suppressing the more aggressive grasses.

uninhibited sexual display. For that is what it was, nothing more or less. Sex from one end of the meadow to the other.

It was colourful sex, too. Over much of the country, though not everywhere, meadow saxifrage was one of the first to open its four big, white petals with greenish lines. It appears in April. Hot behind it, yellow rattle starts flowering in May.Its flowers form racemes on stems up to fifty centimetres (twenty inches) tall and seem harmless on the surface. This is a deceptive plant, however, because below ground its roots are stealing nutrients from its neighbours. Such parasitic dishonesty is less reprehensible than it may seem because it checks the growth of some of the more aggressive plants, thereby allowing the smaller and weaker to flourish and increasing the number of species – the biodiversity – in the meadow. It holds its seeds loose in a papery capsule so they rattle when the breeze shakes them, hence the other part of the plant's name.

Like most of the meadow herbs, yellow rattle benefited from the traditional way hay was made. The grass was mowed, then a horse- or tractor-drawn tedder tossed and turned it to aerate it, leaving the grass in long windrows to dry.

Later, workers with rakes turned the grass to ensure even drying. Haymaking scattered the herb seeds very effectively, while hiding them from the hungry beaks of seed-eating birds and thus ensuring the next generation.

Meadow vetchling appears about the same time as the yellow rattle, its yellow flowers resembling those of peas and beans, which is not surprising because it's a member of the pea family, sometimes called meadow pea, and its black seeds form in pods. The plant has a straggling stem that allows it to clamber over other plants, and its flowers attract bees and wasps.

The rock rose, or common rock rose, for the plant has many close relatives, is another to open its terminal clusters of yellow flowers in May. The flowers have five petals, five sepals and bright orange stamens, and though each individual flower lives for only a short time the plant produces a succession of them through to September. They attract butterflies and moths and they do look a little like roses. The plant itself is another straggler.

June is very definitely summer, even if the weather is still playing at winter, and the archetypal flower of summer is the ox-eye daisy, standing atop a stem almost a metre (about three feet) tall. The capitulum – remember the capitulum? – is about five centimetres (two inches) across, with about twenty white ray florets surrounding its yellow disc florets. People cultivate this daisy, but it has become an invasive weed in some parts of the world where it has been introduced. Its American victims complain that each flower produces up to two hundred seeds and each plant can produce up to forty flower-bearing stems. That's eight thousand seeds per plant. You can see the problem. It's a wonder Americans don't live in an ox-eyed daisy world. You can eat the unopened flower buds, by the way. They're rather like capers.

Columbine or aquilegia, sometimes called granny's bonnet, is another group of summer plants, sixty or seventy species of them, which are widely cultivated. The arrangement of their petals is vaguely reminiscent of an eagle's claw and the Latin for eagle is *aquila*, hence one of its names, while columba is the Latin for dove, the name columbine referring to the supposed resemblance of its groups of flowers to groups of five doves. Columbines have distinctive spurs of varying lengths in which nectar is stored and to reach this an insect or bird must have a tongue, beak or other appendage of the right length. When the head of an insect or bird is pushed into the spur to obtain the nectar, parts of its body come into contact with pollen-covered anthers positioned above the spurs and this is carried to other plants to achieve cross-pollination.

Red clover flowers from May to October. Clovers are legumes, their roots harbouring nodules containing colonies of bacteria which convert nitrogen gas into soluble ammonia that plant roots can absorb, in return for which the plant supplies the bacteria with a share of the nutrients that it synthesizes. When the clover dies it leaves the soil enriched with nitrogen, so farmers grow it as a green manure, a kind of living fertilizer. Some studies have shown that introducing honeybees can significantly increase crop yields. Anyone thinking of doing this needs to know that red clover is predominantly pollinated by long-tongued honeybees because short-tongued species can't reach the nectar – although they sometimes cheat and 'rob' the nectar by biting through the petals. Red clover is very nutritious. Cattle and sheep love it, but farmers take care that they don't eat too much because if they do they'll swell up with bloat, for which the alarming remedy is to puncture the abdomen to release the accumulated gas. Wood mice also eat it (but probably don't get bloat) and bumblebees feed on its nectar. It's an all-round good plant, therefore, and one with a wide range of medicinal uses.

The common poppy, also called the field poppy and corn poppy, can colour a meadow bright red throughout much of the summer and into autumn. When most of the other meadow plants disappeared from the ploughed-up meadows and improved pastures the poppies survived, returning year after year to taunt the farmer. On top of hairy stems up to seventy centimetres (twenty-seven inches) tall, the four-

Papaver Rhœas 293

The corn, field, or common poppy (*Papaver rhoeas*)
can colour entire meadows with its bright red flowers,
as it did on the First World War battlefields of Flanders.

petalled flowers with a black centre are nothing if not dramatic. They owe their tenacity to their seeds, which can remain dormant in the soil for up to forty years, germinating whenever the soil is disturbed. It was the disturbance of the battlefield soils that produced the poppies of Flanders fields immortalized by the Canadian Lieutenant-Colonel John McCrae in one of the most famous poems of the First World War, 'In Flanders Fields':

'In Flanders fields the poppies grow
Between the crosses, row on row . . .'

Farmers hate to see poppies in their arable fields as that makes them appear sloppy and inefficient in the eyes of their neighbours. But they can't win. The poppy appears whenever the soil is cultivated and it's able to flower and set seed before harvest time. It's one of nature's winners.

Red campion is altogether gentler, its five-petalled flowers, about two centimetres (three-quarters of an inch) in size, borne on a smooth stem up to ninety centimetres (three feet) tall. The petals are notched at the outer margin, sometimes so deeply that there seem to be ten of them. Bumblebees and butterflies seek their nectar and moth caterpillars eat the leaves. The closely related white campion often grows side by side with red campion and the two sometimes hybridize to produce pink flowers. Red campion has separate male and female plants and sometimes you may see a female flower coated with a kind of froth. This is to catch pollen and it gives the plant its generic name, *Silene*, referring to Silenus. In ancient Greece Silenus was the god of the wine press, which was how he managed to cover himself with froth. He was also, and probably inevitably, the god of drunkenness and a tutor, and some say foster-father, to Dionysus, the Greek god of wine. The two companions once became separated in the land of Phrygia, but the king of that land, Midas, found Dionysus and treated him hospitably. As a reward, Dionysus conferred on the king the gift that everything he touched would turn to gold. As you know, if it looks too good to be true it probably is and that gift started to go wrong when the food on the table and the king's daughter all turned to gold. But I don't suppose Dionysus or Silenus were that bothered.

Fighting its corner for pollinators is the deep blue cornflower, which is often seen heavy with bees. It's a member of the aster family, its inflorescence a capitulum with two rings of ray florets, those in the outer ring much longer. It used to be a troublesome weed in cereal crops, hence its name, but unlike the poppy it hasn't withstood the intensification of farming. The plough and the herbicides have almost done for it and it's now quite rare. Few plants are more loaded with symbolism than the cornflower. In parts of northern Europe it symbolizes bread, made from the corn amid which it grew, or social and political liberalism. In France it's the flower sold on Remembrance Day, reminiscent of the blue of the French soldiers' uniforms. It's also a symbol of Prussia. And you can eat it – if you can find it. But you mustn't dig it up. To compensate, many gardeners grow cornflowers, which they may know as bachelor's buttons and which they're free to eat to their heart's content.

Most meadow flowers have more than one common name. Another member of the pea family is known to some people as granny's toenails, to others as eggs and bacon or butter and eggs or hen and chickens. Its more dignified, Sunday-go-to-meeting name is bird's foot trefoil. It has clusters of wee yellow flowers and seedpods that look like a bird's foot, as you'd expect. A low-growing plant, it adds splashes of colour to the meadow and joins the pollination party all through the summer.

Enough of all this plant-on-plant love. Did you know agrimony used to go by the name 'lover of people' on account of its therapeutic qualities? The name agrimony is from the Greek *argemone*, applied to any plant that healed the eyes. It's also called church steeples because of its tall flower spikes (some reaching one metre [about three feet] at the height of summer). If neither of those appeal, try calling it

The foxglove (*Digitalis purpurea*), growing up to two
metres (over six feet) tall, is possibly the most familiar
flower of the summer meadows and roadsides.

sticklewort, burr marigold, or cockeburr, all of which are richly deserved because once pollinated its seeds are contained in little vessels covered in hooks that cling to anything that brushes against them.

The true perfume of summer begins to fill the air in June and continues into September as the meadowsweet, the queen of the meadow, reaches its full height of more than one metre (about three feet) and opens its cymes of cream-white flowers. It's one of the plants the Druids considered sacred. Both foliage and blossoms are sweetly scented and the plant was once strewn on floors to improve the air in rooms and in churches at summer festivals and weddings – one of its names is bridewort. In *The Herball, or general historie of plantes*, published in 1597, the herbalist John Gerard wrote:

> 'The leaves and floures of Meadowsweet farre excelle all other strowing herbs for to decke up houses, to strawe in chambers, halls and banqueting-houses in the summer-time, for the smell thereof makes the heart merrie and joyful and delighteth the senses.'

It cares nothing for our merrie and joyful hearts, of course. The purpose of the sweet perfume is to attract clouds of insects seeking its pollen. The flowers produce no nectar, but a surplus of pollen to feed the flies, thrips and bumblebees that pay for their meal by transporting pollen to the female flowers. Could its perfume sweeten the aromas around a barbecue? It might be worth a try.

Meadowsweet is edible and is still used to flavour drinks, especially ale and mead – it's sometimes called meadwort. It will also add a delicate almond flavour to jams and stewed fruit. It has many medicinal uses and is a dyeplant, producing yellow, red, or black depending on the mordant used.

Foxgloves flower at about the same time as the meadowsweet. They are possibly the most familiar of the meadow flowers, at least partly because of their size and abundance. Growing up to two metres (over six feet) tall, with simple racemes of purple, pink, or white tubular flowers, you can't miss them and you can't mistake them for anything else. They're very in your face. Foxgloves secrete an ant repellent, loliodide, at one time used in the Forest of Dean as an insecticide and disinfectant, but bumblebees love them for their nectar and caterpillars of the orange spot and foxglove pug moths eat the flowers; other caterpillars, including those of the lesser yellow underwing, prefer the leaves. Don't you try tasting them, though. All parts of the plant are very poisonous and it has been known to kill people. Death is rare, but consuming even a small amount of foxglove will make you feel dreadful.

You'd think mowing would destroy flowering herbs, but in fact it's essential because it removes the tall grass that would shade and eventually suppress them. Farmers aiming to maximize wildflowers mow the meadow in sections at intervals from June to late August and use it for grazing at other times.

Desert in bloom

—

It is the Earth's orbit of the sun combined with the 23.5-degree tilt in its rotational axis that generates our seasons. Meteorologists also divide up the year into four seasons, but they base them on the annual temperature cycle rather than astronomy. This means the meteorological seasons run approximately three weeks ahead of the astronomical seasons. The dates vary a bit from year to year, but in 2015 the meteorological spring ran from 1 March until 31 May.

The point is that in mid-latitude temperate zones, leaving aside the woodland frenzy, the spring botanical orgy can be a fairly leisurely event. The plants have no need to rush. They have time to wallow in their debauchery. Lucky them. We must avert our eyes. They know – and I use the term deliberately, because you mustn't suppose plants aren't fully aware of what's going on around them just because you never see one tippy-texting away at a smartphone – that as the days go by the sunshine will strengthen and the rain will fall pretty evenly, so the ground won't dry out. The woodland herbs also know that the trees are getting themselves ready to unfurl their leaves and when that happens they'll have to cope with being in shade. Still, there's time enough for plenty of hanky-panky.

In Britain, we, and those woodland plants, live in a mid-latitude temperate maritime climate. I apologize for using a technical term, but I do so in order to compare this with another, very different climate type: the desert climate. A desert is a dry place, obviously. It's dry because the amount of rain that falls in a year is less than the amount that would evaporate from an open pond, if there were such a thing, during the same period. It doesn't mean rain never falls, only that such rain as moistens the ground is soon lost by evaporation. What does dry mean? Well, Iquique, Peru, once went for four years with no rain at all and in July of the fifth year there was a shower that delivered 15 millimetres. Over a period of 21 years Iquique received an annual average of 1.5 millimetres of rain. That's dry. Even most deserts aren't quite that dry. Tamanrasset, in southern Algeria, positively soggy by comparison, receives an annual average of about 50 millimetres. Just to put that in perspective, Central Park in New York receives an annual average of about 1130 millimetres.

Desert rain isn't spread evenly through the year. There's usually a rainy season and during the rainy season there can be torrential downpours. I know you wouldn't be so foolhardy, but I must warn you that next time you're crossing a desert in the rainy season on no account should you camp in a dry riverbed.

A desert is a tough place but there are compensations if you're a plant adapted to cope with it. First, there's not much competition for nutrients and second, there's no lack of sunshine. There's just the miserly rainfall to deal with and there are ways around that. You might dispense with leaves, allow your stems to swell and store water, and/or let the stems take charge of photosynthesis. Use sharp spines to ward off animals that might fancy you for lunch, make the water you store poisonous as an extra precaution, and you've turned yourself into a cactus (if you're American) or a euphorbia (if you're African). Or you could shed your leaves at the start of the dry season, use young branches for photosynthesis and shed them if conditions get too harsh, and be ready to grow leaves and flowers the instant the rain returns.

The Atacama Desert in Chile, blooming after a fall of rain. At intervals of four or five years hundreds of square kilometres of bare rock and sand are transformed into a floral wonderland that changes colour as plants flower and disappear, with others taking their place.

Alternatively you could avoid the dry weather altogether. How? By spending almost all of your time as a seed, waiting in the ground for your chance. To succeed at that you'll need to grab the chance while it's there. No leisurely dalliance for you, nor time for subtlety. It's up, shout as loud as you can for an insect, any insect will do, and get it all over with before your surroundings turn back into a pile of dust.

Deserts appear barren, but if you take a sample of dry desert soil and sift it very carefully you'll find it contains hundreds or even thousands of seeds. These are waiting to be moistened and they have to be prepared for a long wait. In the California deserts, for instance, evening primrose seeds can wait, dried out and dormant, for fifty years or more. If patience is a virtue, the evening primrose deserves a medal. The reward, of course, is to be moistened. When that happens the desert is suddenly carpeted in its yellow flowers.

How fast can the waiting plants respond? In southern Africa, red spiderling, also called spreading hogweed, can germinate its stored seeds, open its big, bright flowers and set seed all in the space of ten days. After a week or two it's all over and there's no sign of them – unless you sift the soil for their seeds.

Chile is the country in which to watch the most magnificent desert display. The spectacle occurs in parts of the Atacama Desert every four or five years, usually beginning in August and lasting until November or sometimes December.

The desert cauliflower or pillow cushion plant of the Sahara is dome-shaped and looks rather like a green cauliflower. It's no great beauty but, like Archilochus's hedgehog, it has one trick and it does it very well. Bursting into action the moment it feels moisture, the seed germinates within ten minutes, sends a root downward and a shoot upward, opens its seed leaves (cotyledons) and commences photosynthesis, the entire process to this point taking ten hours.

"Seed of the desert cauliflower germinates within ten minutes of sensing rain or moisture."

Then there's bindweed, or convolvulus. As every gardener knows, if its roots anchor themselves, before you know it the tendrils are everywhere, across the ground and up and through any plant it meets. Then it opens its trumpet-shaped flowers in mockery. If it's a problem in gardens, imagine how it behaves in the Sahara Desert. It goes mad, completing its entire life cycle in six weeks or less.

The eyelash plant (*Blepharis ciliaris*), another Saharan native, stores its seeds on the dead, dry plant itself, in capsules each containing two seeds, the seeds and the seed coats both covered in hairs. The seeds are attached to the capsule in such a way that when it rains and water enters the capsule the tension pulling the two halves of the capsule apart overcomes the capsule's strength and it explodes, hurling out its seeds, which fly several metres if it is rain that moistens the capsule and more than one hundred metres if the plant is in a river bed that floods, ensuring that the seeds don't drown. As soon as the seeds land their hairs absorb moisture, which makes them swell and pull the seeds until they're at an angle to the soil surface and in close contact with the soil, allowing the root from the germinating seed to penetrate. The root can grow nearly five centimetres (two inches) in the first 24 hours after being moistened. But the eyelash plant hasn't exhausted its repertoire. In some *Blepharis* species (for there are about one hundred), if a seed falls into a river, within a few minutes it covers itself with a layer of mucilage that prevents it from germinating under water or being damaged by abrasion as the flowing torrent bashes it across the stony bed. Other *Blepharis* species germinate on the riverbed, which, after all, will soon be dry once more. Even then, the plant remains cautious. Wetting the plant causes only about one-third of the capsules to fire their seeds into the outside world. The remainder dry out when the rain ceases and the tension within the capsule is restored. So the plant releases its seeds a few at a time with each fall of rain.

The eyelash plant (*Blepharis ciliaris*, also called *Acanthodium delilli* and *Acanthus delilli*) has fierce thorns and bright blue flowers. It thrives in the Sahara, Arabia, and the Middle East.

1. *RUELLIA persica*.
2. *ACANTHUS ciliaris*.

There are also plants that produce seeds of different types. For example, one of the seepweeds, *Suaeda corniculata*, which grows in salt soils in the deserts of Asia, produces large brown seeds and small black seeds, thereby giving itself two shots at germinating, depending on the conditions. The brown seeds germinate rapidly and don't become dormant in the soil, so if conditions are favourable, they get on with producing new plants. The black seeds, on the other hand, remain dormant in the soil and won't germinate as long as it remains dry and salty. When the rains fall, moistening them and washing away some of the salt, the black seeds germinate.

"Suaeda corniculata *produces two different types of seed, which allows it two shots at germination.*"

Sand button (*Neurada procumbens*) also gives itself multiple opportunities for germination, and it has an ingenious way of distributing its seeds. The plant grows in deserts from North Africa all the way to Pakistan and India. Its fruits – the buttons that lie in the sand – are disc-shaped and smooth on the underside but covered with small spines on the upper side. When an animal treads on one, or a vehicle drives over it, the fruit sticks to the foot or tyre and is transported away from the parent plant until, after a time, it falls off. Each fruit contains several seeds. When the fruit is moistened it opens and one seed germinates, quickly extending a root vertically downward into the wet sand. If the moisture resulted from nothing more than a brief shower, the soil will dry before the seed has had time to extend its shoot and seed leaves so it can begin photosynthesis, in which case the root will wither and die. No matter, because the next fall of rain will trigger germination in another seed and the process will repeat. It will go on repeating until either the fruit runs out of seeds or one of the seeds makes it, and a new plant emerges.

Gymnarrhena micrantha (it has no common name) belongs to the aster family and also has an insurance policy to ensure survival of the next generation. It increases its chance of reproducing by producing different kinds of flower. It's a small plant that grows no more than three centimetres (one inch) tall and it lives in the Sahara and deserts of the Near East. It produces two kinds of capitula. One type develops below ground, its ray florets forming a small tube that projects just above ground. Each of these inflorescences produces one or two fruits that remain attached to their mother plant, which dies once it has set seed. The seeds below ground are protected from seed-eating animals, especially ants, and they remain dormant until rain moistens them and they germinate. The other capitula open above ground on the tips of up to three branches about three centimetres (one inch) long. These produce fruits with long hairs, like dandelion seeds, and they also remain attached to the mother plant, protected inside tough buds where the ants can't reach them. The following winter the first shower of rain soaks and softens the bracts and all the pods open. That's when the ants attack, but before they have time to scoff the lot, the wind catches the hairs and carries the seeds away.

Dispersing seeds reduces competition between the new seedlings and between seedlings and their parent. This is obviously sensible. Sooner or later you have to kick them out of the nest, after all, or you'll never have any peace and your bank account will wither. If you're a plant, and rooted to the spot, the kicking out has to happen while they're still seeds. It sounds cruel, but you know it's for their own good and, anyway, can you think of an alternative?

There are ways to do this. You can produce seeds like the sand button that cling to passers-by or you can fit them out with long hairs, called a pappus, and wait for them to waft away on the desert breeze to who knows where. Or you can be proactive about it and scatter them yourself. Chances are that if that's the strategy you adopt they'll call you tumbleweed and they'll hire you to appear in Hollywood Westerns. First you have to die, which is a bit of a downer, and as you die and shrivel you detach your roots and curl your stems and leaves into a ball with the seeds on the inside. Then the wind will blow you this way and that, along the streets of the ghost towns while they play mournful music, and without the camera noticing you'll scatter your seeds as you go.

There's also a North African and Middle Eastern equivalent, called the rose of Jericho, despite being a member of the cabbage family and not a rose at all, or, for that matter, having much to do with Jericho. It works in the same way as the Wild West tumble weed, curling up as it shrivels and scattering seeds as it rolls along, but with one difference: the shrivelled plant uncurls if it becomes moist. For that reason people buy the dried plant as a house ornament that doubles as a kind of hygrometer, responding to changes in air humidity. It makes a talking point, unless everyone has one.

There's even one desert seed-scatterer that rates a mention in the Old Testament:

> 'And one went out into the field to gather herbs, and found a wild vine, and gathered thereof wild gourds his lap full, and came and shred them into the pot of pottage: for they knew *them* not.

> 'So they poured out for the men to eat. And it came to pass, as they were eating of the pottage, that they cried out, and said, O thou man of God, *there* is death in the pot. And they could not eat *thereof*.'
>
> (2 Kings, 4, 39–40)

They'd gathered what's known as the colocynth, vine of Sodom, bitter apple, bitter cucumber, and desert gourd. A close relative of the watermelon, *Citrullus colocynthis* has extremely bitter, gourd-like fruits about the size of an orange. The edible seeds are highly nutritious and the dried pulp is used as a laxative, but the bitterness is enough to put most people off. Left to its own devices the fruit rolls around in the wind

The dried-up rose of Jericho (*Anastatica hierochuntica*) rolls along the ground scattering its seeds, but if it becomes moist the plant unfolds and comes back to life. For that reason it's known as a resurrection plant.

until it comes to rest against rocks or is trapped in soft sand. There it shrivels and its tiny seeds wait for the next rain to moisten them.

Now that travel to remote places is relatively straightforward, many of us will visit a real desert. We might expect a barren landscape of bare rock and dust, or of high sand dunes, and most of the time we'll not be disappointed. That is what the desert looks like. But now and then, for a few weeks or a month or two maybe once in ten years, a deluge of rain transforms the scenery. Then the visitor will see a blaze of colour, the colours changing every week or two as flowers complete their life cycles and others take their place. The flowers are bright and loud to attract the insects that also emerge in response to the moisture and fly among them, each in search of its favourites. And the emergence of the insects brings out those that hunt insects: the spiders, scorpions, small rodents, and reptiles that hunt the hunters. For that brief space the desert comes fully to life. Then it ends. The plants vanish, their seeds safely stored below ground, and the animals find shelter from the hot sun, emerging only at twilight and through the night. By day the landscape appears lifeless once more. But that sudden show of flowering and reproduction gives the lie to the usual face the desert presents to the world. You may not see much evidence, but the desert is very far from dead.

Through the insect's eye
—

'It's a sight for sore eyes,' garden-lovers agree as they gaze in admiration at the long summer flower borders and take photographs to pore over during the dark winter evenings.

Those are two of the ways to view flowers, and there are others. Insects view a flower border not as a pretty picture, but as a map, marked out with routes that guide them to brightly visible destinations that offer food. The whole scene is shown in colours quite different from those which you and I see, and includes some colours we don't see at all.

Surfaces reflect light that falls on them, but most surfaces reflect only part of it, absorbing the rest. Sunlight is colourless because it comprises radiation with a range of wavelengths – a waveband – that add up to white. So a surface that reflects the full waveband will be white. Pass the white light through a prism, or cloud droplets, and the different wavelengths separate into violet, indigo, blue, green, yellow, orange, and red – the colours of the rainbow. When white light strikes a surface and certain of its wavelengths are absorbed, the effect is to remove from the light the colours associated with those wavelengths. Robert Burns wrote: 'O my love is like a red, red rose that's newly sprung in June.' What he really meant to write was: 'O my love is like a rose that absorbs all the wavelengths of light from violet to orange, leaving only red to be reflected that's newly sprung in June.' Only he couldn't get it to scan so he had to simplify it. Poetry is difficult.

The reflected light, which is the part of the white light that hasn't been absorbed, enters our eyes and is focused on to the retina at the rear of the eye. And at this point you realize that light is a bit odd. It travels around the universe as waves of radiation but it's also made up of photons, which are discrete particles. The wavelength of the radiation, which there are instruments to measure, corresponds to the energy possessed by the photons. When the photons strike light-sensitive cells in the retina their energy generates impulses that travel to a part of the brain where some, sent by rod cells, are interpreted as monochrome light and shade, while those from cone cells correspond to the energies or wavelengths of red, green, and blue. The brain merges these into what we perceive as colour. Colour, then, is something of an abstract concept. To a large extent it's constructed in the brain. Is the red, red rose red at all?

A camera imitates our vision. It has to do so, obviously, because otherwise no one would buy it. Reflected light passes through lenses to be focused on light-sensitive surfaces where the different energies of the photons are interpreted in ways that our eyes perceive as the colours of the original.

Now we have another problem. If we all agree that Burns's rose was red, can we be sure that what I call red is the same as what you call red? Well, no we can't. That's because we're all different. To be more precise, the colour-sensitive cone cells in our retinas have a bit of wiggle room. My red cones might fire their impulses at a slightly different energy level than yours. If the differences become fairly large, we have to make judgements. If the majority of people say the object is red and I say it's orange or green, because those are the cones that are activated in my eyes, then we go with the consensus and everybody turns on me and tells me I'm colour blind. People who design cameras and television sets go with the consensus.

Gardens, deserts, forests and ice sheets, all are bathed in sunlight – solar radiation – that's absorbed and reflected by the surfaces it strikes. It would be exceedingly odd, therefore, if living organisms didn't find ways to make use of it. Plants are sensitive to light, especially red light, and to changing light duration and intensity, but they don't have eyes. Almost all animals, on the other hand, do possess eyes, but they are eyes of widely different kinds. At their simplest they simply detect light and shade and the direction of the light source. At their most advanced, an eagle circling high above the mountainside, borne on a rising air current, is watching the ground to spot the grazing rabbit that has wandered too far from its burrow or a small rodent whose scurrying disturbs the vegetation. The evolution of eyes was inevitable once a predator was able to see its prey clearly enough to chase it and the prey was able to see the predator coming. All of these different eyes detect light in the same way, but as the animals evolved, many different constructions emerged. More than ninety per cent of animals possess eyes, the exceptions being those that live in permanent and absolute darkness, but eyes are not all made the same way.

It's possible, therefore, or even likely, that the visitors enjoying the colours and plant arrangements in the borders each see things slightly differently. What is absolutely certain is that the insects among the flowers have a very different view of their world.

head

eye

thorax

abdomen

An insect's eyes are very large in proportion to the size of its head.

As the illustration shows, compared with ours an insect's eyes are very large as a proportion of the size of the head. They also bulge, giving them a wide field of vision, although this doesn't show very well in the side-on view. And their structure is quite different from that of our eyes. Our eyes are simple, while those of an insect – and also a spider, scorpion, shrimp, crab, and all other arthropods – are compound. All 'simple' means is that our mammalian eyes consist of a single organ, while those of an arthropod consist of many individual parts.

The individual parts are called ommatidia and the number varies from one species to another. Silverfish eyes have just a few, while a dragonfly's eye has approximately thirty thousand. Silverfish live in dark nooks and crannies, but dragonflies seize their prey on the wing, so they need acute vision.

At its outer end, each ommatidium has a transparent cornea and below it there is a cone with a crystalline structure. Between them the cornea and cone focus the incoming light on to a rod, called the rhabdom, made of and surrounded by light-detecting cells, all linked to optic nerves at the base. In insects that are active by day, pigment cells surround the ommatidium, isolating it from the neighbouring ommatidia. Nocturnal insects lack the pigment cells, so their ommatidia can receive light from their neighbours.

Each ommatidium contributes a single point, like a pixel, to the overall image. The insect's brain merges these 'pixels' to make a continuous image, just as our eyes merge the pixels in a digital image, but there's another effect. An ommatidium is active only while light is shining directly down it and it's unable to move independently, so if the light source moves across the eye it creates a flicker as the ommatidia fire in succession, which the insect detects instantly and to which it can respond very fast. When you aim to swat a housefly it sees your swatter coming and takes about one-fiftieth of a second to start moving out of the way, which explains why flies aren't extinct despite our best efforts.

Compound eyes are much less efficient than ours at seeing detail, however. In fact they're about one hundred times less efficient and the only way to compensate for this is to add more ommatidia, which is why insects have such big eyes. Even so, for an insect to see as well as you or I it would need two compound eyes each about twenty metres across. Unwieldy, you'll agree, and I doubt an insect with eyes that big could ever get airborne. Day-flying insects see contrast fairly well in good light, but not so well in very bright light and they generally stop flying when the light fades to evening although some can see well enough to fly by moonlight.

The eyes of nocturnal insects allow them to operate in dim light, but with a loss in perception of detail.

Insects are able to see some colours. Their compound eyes are sensitive to ultraviolet light, which we can't see, and especially sensitive to blue-green light. They see red colours poorly or not at all.

Their different colour perception means that the flowers they visit look quite different from the way they appear to us. The flowers in the border are domesticated. They've been bred and manipulated to produce the vibrant colours people enjoy. Look at wild flowers in the countryside, however, and you'll see lots of whites, yellows, blues, mauves, purples, and some pinks, but not so many strong reds.

Because insect eyes respond to ultraviolet (UV) wavelengths, many people jump to the conclusion that this means UV light is extremely important to insects. It isn't. They do see in UV, but the colour is quite faint and not especially striking. What's really important to an insect is to distinguish between the colour of a flower and the green of the leaves surrounding it.

So insects see colour, but not the colours that we see. Groundsel, for instance, bears what appear to us to be bright yellow flowers. A bee sees them as UV-green, which is a very bright, almost luminescent green that stands out strongly from a background of non-UV colours. Hoary alyssum (*Beteroa incana*), also known as hoary alison, false hoary madwort, and hoary beteroa, is a mustard with white flowers. To a bee the flowers are blue-green. Bird's-foot trefoil bears yellow flowers, but to a bee they are bright green, a colour that stands out against the darker green of the leaves and the many other yellow flowers.

Pink flowers appear blue-green to a bee, and purple and mauve flowers appear blue. Insects don't see red. To them, it appears as a shade of grey or as black, depending on the shade of red. Yet despite this several species of bees, at least one hoverfly, and various beetles and grasshoppers visit the field poppy. The reason is that the insects don't see the flower as red, but as a kind of very deep violet. Brazilian fuchsia (*Justicia rizzinii*), on the other hand (no relation of the true fuchsias), has yellow flowers that shade to red at the base, and bees don't see that red at all; to them the base of the flower is a dull grey. That doesn't matter to the plant, because hummingbirds pollinate it and they can see red just fine.

It's not only the flower colours that insects see differently, of course. They also have a different view of each other. For instance, to eyes sensitive to UV, the yellow Cleopatra butterfly has deep purple hindwings and white forewings with a purple margin. It all goes to show that to an insect the world looks very altered from our perception of it, and flowers are designed for insects and other pollinators, not people.

Many flowers provide potential pollinators with visual guides – called nectar or pollen guides – to help them alight securely or to guide them to the nectar and pollen. Some of these are visible to us. The lower side of pink foxglove petals have dark dots outlined in white, and in white foxgloves the markings are dark red. Petals of eyebright have dark lines above and below to guide insects in and pansies are one of many flowers with lines apparently radiating from the centre but in fact leading insects towards it.

Other flowers have guides we can't see because they're visible only to eyes sensitive to UV. Monkey-flowers (*Mimulus*) are yellow with darker spots forming a faint nectar guide, but under UV light the flower is light blue with a much darker blue centre forming the guide. Orange coneflowers (*Rudbeckia fulgida*), which are composites related to asters and daisies, have yellow ray florets surrounding yellow disc florets. To a bee, however, the outer tips of the ray florets appear yellow, the inner part green, each floret has a bright yellow spot near the base, and each disc floret has a yellow spot. A butterfly sees the flower differently from a bee, with very pale mauve tips to the ray florets and the inner part of the inflorescence brown, though the yellow spots look the same. Marsh marigolds are bright yellow, but in UV light the petals are dark blue with pale blue borders. Very many flowers use guides to help approaching insects, and the guides do even more. They help deter nectar thieves. We'll meet them later.

This is all very well in daylight, but after the plant-lovers have headed for the car park and home, the gates are closed and darkness falls, life in the garden must go on.

For many small creatures, darkness means safety from predators, and they're able to move around perfectly well. There's a Central American sweat bee, for example, that nests in a hollowed-out twig in the undergrowth and can find its way in the dark through the rainforest to a nocturnal flower, enjoy its supper, then find its way back home with no trouble at all. It does this by means of remembered landmarks, though its brain is no bigger than a grain of rice. An Australian bull ant feeds on nocturnal flowers, travelling confidently on foot from its nest to the flower and back home. Obviously, nocturnal insects can see in very poor light. They're able to do so because their eyes accumulate the impulses from arriving photons until the signal is strong enough to form an image. A cockroach can see when its eyes receive no more than one photon of light every ten seconds, but the image it perceives is very vague and blurry. It's enough, though, to allow it to dodge your foot, and so far as the roach is concerned that's good enough.

Some flowers fold in their petals and close down for the night, but others open for the night-time pollinators. The flowers are most commonly white, because colours don't show well at night. But to complicate things for the night-flying moths, when the wind blows the flowers wave about. They don't even have the common decency to stand still to be fertilized.

However, a bit of waving in the breeze doesn't deter the Carolina sphinx moth (*Manduca texta*) which is a hawkmoth the size of a hummingbird. Its caterpillar, known as the tobacco hookworm or goliath worm, dines on leaves but the adult feeds exclusively on nectar, at night. What's more it feeds on the wing, hovering, while its target sways from side to side. Simon Sponberg and colleagues at the University of Washington set up an experiment to see what was happening. They discovered that at two different light levels, one representing early dusk and the other a quarter-moon, the hovering moth moved from side to side, matching the movement of its flower, provided the flower swayed back and forth no more than about twice each second. If the flower moved faster the moth was unable to track it, especially at the lower light level. Its eyes accumulate photons, like the roach's, so it can't track the motion of the flower very precisely, but its tracking is accurate at the speed with which flowers usually move. So the moth synchronizes its lateral movements with the motion of the breeze-tossed flower. And it gets its supper.

The Carolina sphinx moth (*Manduca texta*) feeds on nectar of the nightshade family at night and is able to track the movement of the flower as it blows around despite poor vision.

CHAPTER 2

TARTS AND HOOKERS

Meet the flowers that are wide open and available to all insect life. These plants are not in the least fussy about who tramps across them – they are the trollops of the hedge and herb garden.

Shapes
and sizes
—

Flowers come in a range of colours, but colour isn't the only means they have to show that they're different from other species. They also present a variety of sizes and shapes, the latter determining which animals they prefer to pollinate them. Think of cymes or the globose heads of buddleia inflorescences and compare those with the open, rather flat flowers of sunflowers, buttercups, or poppies. Clearly, pretty well any flying insect has access to an open, flat flower that shamelessly exposes its reproductive apparatus for all the world to see. An insect can just walk across it. But only insects with long tongues can reach inside buddleia flowers and not every insect could or would want to clamber inside the trumpet of a wild daffodil. It might wonder (if insects go in much for wondering) whether there's room inside to turn around and whether it would be able to get out.

Up to a point, therefore, the shape of a flower or, more precisely, the arrangement of its petals, the corolla, provides a clue to the type of pollinators it attracts. If the corolla is wide open you can expect it to lure many pollinator species. Pick a sunny summer's day and spend an hour or two watching the asters, or the umbels of angelica, celery, dill or wild umbellifers along rural roadsides. If you're patient it won't be long before you see bees, hoverflies, flies, gnats, mosquitoes, and all sorts of other flying insects visiting these inflorescences. You may even spot beetles, because it's not difficult for the heavyweights of the insect world to land on and walk across the florets making up a fairly solid umbel. These flowers are wide open, available to all. They're not in the least fussy about who tramps across them. Trollops of the hedge and herb garden, you might say. Take the Persian or pink silk tree, a member of the bean family from southwestern and eastern Asia that is grown widely for ornament. Butterflies

This female three-spot grass yellow butterfly (*Eurema blanda*) is laying its eggs on young leaves of a Persian silk tree (*Albizia julibrissin*), a native of eastern and southwestern Asia, but widely grown elsewhere. The butterfly may well have pollinated the tree's flowers, which also attract bees and hummingbirds.

and bees in Asia and hummingbirds in America pollinate its flowers and in its natural home, caterpillars of the three-spot grass yellow butterfly feed on its leaves.

And that, you might think, makes a lot of sense if you're a plant. The object, after all, is to transfer pollen from one flower to another, so the more visitors you attract the better. It doesn't matter in the least what sort of animal does the transferring, any one of them will do – but that comes with a downside. There's absolutely no point in going to all the trouble of producing pollen if that pollen is going to end up wasted inside a flower of an entirely different species. And that's the trouble. A flower that's open to all will be visited by all, and that's true of every plant that adopts this strategy. Although the flower will certainly succeed in dispersing its pollen, there's no guarantee whatever that the pollen will reach a female plant of the same species. The insects couldn't care less, after all. What's it to them if sunflowers are trying to mate with parsnips? So in this fix there's only one thing the flowers can do, and that's to produce copious quantities of pollen and be prepared for most of it to be wasted. Provided one insect carries your pollen to a female flower of your species, resulting in the fertilization of the female, seeds will be produced and you'll have reproduced successfully.

That's all you need. Life can go on. So producing open, easily accessible flowers works, but it's inefficient because it means the plant must expend a much greater proportion of its energy and nutrient resources in producing pollen than would be the case if it were more selective in its choice of pollinators.

In some circumstances this might not matter. Think of the bonny purple heather that romantically carpets the hillsides of the Scottish Highlands. On the nutrient-poor acid soils where heather grows it tends to take over, so when heather pollen is moved it is very likely to reach another heather flower. The flowers attract bumblebees and honeybees, which are the most efficient pollinators, but also flies, especially big ones, and butterflies. There aren't all that many flying insects out on the bleak, wet, windy moors and hillsides, so the heather can't afford to be too choosy.

Big, blousy sunflowers also tend to grow in dense stands and they're so tall that there are not many places for pollen to go, except from one sunflower to another nearby, so the open-door policy suits them well. Butterflies, beetles and flies pollinate sunflowers, but bees of many species are the most common visitors. The ray florets of the sunflower capitulum form a guide, directing the pollinator toward the disc florets. In the sunflower there are up to two thousand of these and they open one row at a time, starting at the outside and working toward the centre. Each floret opens first as a male, projecting its anthers above the rim, and later as a female, the style pushing upward and the lobes of the stigma spreading out.

If you were a plant that decided to specialize in your choice of insect pollinator you might aim to attract bees. It's a popular choice. There are lots of them around, so this shouldn't be too difficult. Making your flowers bilaterally symmetrical would be a good way to start. This means that if you were to draw an imaginary line from top to bottom across the corolla the two sides of the line would be mirror images of each other. Many orchid flowers are bilaterally symmetrical, as are sweet peas, snapdragons, and many more. This shape helps the bee orientate itself as it approaches, so it arrives at the right angle. If you make the flower tubular, the bee will happily push its way inside, knowing it can exit safely in reverse, so this is even better, and because the bee is enclosed by the fused petals, it's bound to pick up a goodly dusting of pollen. You can add a final refinement by colouring your petals or sepals purple or blue, which are the colours bees see best.

The sunflower is a composite, open to all insect pollinators, but especially popular among bees of all kinds. Note the rings in the disc, formed as the florets develop one row at a time.

The purple flowerheads of field scabious (*Knautia arvensis*) attract bees, as well as hoverflies and butterflies, but in this case there's a difference, because the pollinators include one specialist, the scabious bee (*Andrena hattorfiana*), and both plant and bee are in difficulty. The plant flowers from July to September, but the flower meadows in which it grows are often grazed and then cut for hay before the flowers appear, so there are fewer flowers than there once were. The scabious bee raises its young exclusively on pollen from the field scabious and in recent years the population of the bee has been in decline, possibly due at least in part to the decline in the number of scabious flowers. At the same time, the scabious bee is the most efficient pollinator of the flower, and the bee's decline may have caused a decline in the plant. The field scabious is by no means rare, but its numbers are believed to be decreasing. One thing leads to another and it's all connected. That's ecology for you.

Changes in farming practices make a difference. Years ago farmers grew peas and beans to feed livestock and wild members of the pea and bean family were a familiar sight growing in and beside fields. Fields of peas and beans are less common these days and more intensive management of pastures has reduced populations of their wild relatives. It may be no coincidence, therefore, that the bees which once specialized in pollinating them are also reduced in numbers.

Going back to pollination strategies though, you might decide to produce flowers for butterflies. Now you can be truly picky, by making your corolla into a tube that matches the length of the tongue of your favourite butterfly. Butterflies are especially fond of thistles and knapweeds.

Or how about setting your cap at moths? To succeed there it's best to have white flowers that show up better in the dark, and you may as well close them up during the day so you don't risk wasting pollen. Try releasing a sweet perfume. Moths have a keen sense of smell.

In days of yore, but not so long ago either, there lived among us a number of botanical nationalists who hated all plants that had not grown naturally in their own country, possibly in their own back yards, since before time began. These puritanical folk developed a deep abhorrence for the buddleia, introduced to Britain in the 1890s. Apart from being vulgarly festooned with flowers its seeds are dispersed by the wind, so it grows almost anywhere and can be invasive. So down with it! Or rather up with it and away to the bonfire. Then conservationists, famed for their inordinate fondness for butterflies, noticed that the insects they so admired were all over the festooning mauve flowers, so much so that they started calling buddleia the butterfly bush. It's not only butterflies that pollinate them. They also attract bees and moths and a variety has been bred in North America to be pollinated by hummingbirds. So nowadays we've all grown up and butterfly bushes are *de rigeur* in the conservationist's garden. They also flourish along the sides of railway cuttings, no doubt to much lepidopteran rejoicing.

If you were tempted by the idea of moth pollinators, why not go a couple of steps further and recruit bats? They're nocturnal, of course, so you'll be best off with white or pale flowers, but you need to remember that, small though most of them are, bats are much bigger than the moths they hunt, so your flowers will need to be bigger to accommodate them, and preferably bell-shaped so a bat can wriggle inside. Bats pollinate several hundred species of plants, including mangoes, guavas, agave, and wild (but not cultivated and edible) bananas. There's even a bat that specializes in wild bananas. Would you believe it's called the banana bat (*Musonycteris harrisoni*)? It has a very long snout and a tongue almost as long as its body to reach to the base of the flower. In fact the tongue is so long it won't fit in the bat's mouth, so it's carried in a groove on its chest. The banana bat occurs only on the western side of Central America; elsewhere in the world wild bananas are pollinated by other bat species and by birds.

"The tongue of the banana bat is so long it carries it in a groove on its chest."

All a pollinator has to do to achieve the plants' purpose is to push its face into a series of flowers, and many animals can do that, even reptiles. A rare and endangered Mauritian plant, *Roussea simplex*, relies for pollination wholly on a lizard, the blue-tailed day-gecko (*Phelsuma cepediana*), found only in Mauritius and also rare. It's an odd plant, a climber that also forms a shrub, its flowers with thick, fleshy, orange petals, and an abundant supply of nectar. In seeking the nectar, the gecko thrusts its snout deep into the flower, in the process acquiring a liberal dusting of pollen, which, of course, it carries to the next flower it visits in search of a sweet energy drink. And the collaboration doesn't end there, because the gecko also eats the fruit. This is shaped like the teat on a baby's bottle and the lizard sucks a jelly from it. The jelly contains the seeds, which the lizard swallows and later disperses in its droppings. It's another case of mutual dependence, a beautiful friendship. If the plant disappears it takes the gecko's food supply with it, and the plant can't survive without its gecko.

Geckos are good climbers, and so is the eastern pygmy-possum, a tiny Australian marsupial. It feeds on insects, but much prefers nectar and pollen from banksias, eucalypts, and bottlebrushes. When the flowers are over, the possum is happy to eat the fruits.

Nor is the eastern pygmy-possum the only marsupial pollinator. The eminent, nineteenth-century Austrian botanist Anton Kerner thought it not impossible that kangaroos might be among the animals that pollinate one group of bushes that used to be called *Dryandra* and are now reclassified as *Banksia*. These have flowers arranged around the edge of a kind of cup into which a nutritious liquid flows. The flowers are at about head-height for a kangaroo. They may also attract a species of cuscus, which is a type of possum.

Out on the African plains, giraffes are very fond of the

flowers that grow in the canopy of thorn trees. They browse more than four metres above ground level and walk up to six kilometres a day as they move from one stand of trees to another, their long necks meaning they have little competition from rival browsers. As they bite off the flowers they cover their faces with pollen, which they carry on their fur from flower to flower. And this, you might suppose, is just great. The trees must be delighted to welcome such enthusiastic helpers. Only it's not simply nectar the giraffes are after. They eat the entire flower and that means it's unable to produce fruit, never mind that it's been pollinated. You can't win. Botanists studying the effect of giraffes on the thorn trees found that flowers higher up, beyond the reach even of the giraffes, produced fruit just fine, with the help of insect pollinators.

The giraffes don't do any serious harm, though. The clusters of flowers comprise mixtures of male, bisexual, and sterile flowers. The giraffes can eat as many sterile flowers as they like without harming the tree, and eating the male flowers won't harm the tree either, provided the giraffes get pollen all over their faces as they do so.

"Out on the African plains, giraffes move around the pollen of thorn trees but in truth are more interested in eating than pollinating."

Mammals also pollinate flowers closer to ground level. The northern vampire cup, for example, is a parasitic South African plant (*Cytinus visseri*) that hides its dark red flowers beneath the shrubs from which it steals food. The flowers release a perfume to attract the small mammals that pollinate it. These include elephant shrews, striped field mice, and pygmy mice.

You wouldn't expect primates, the smartest of the mammals (we're primates, after all), to be left out, would you? Balsa trees grow naturally in tropical Central and South America and by day white-headed (also called white-faced and white-throated) capuchin monkeys pollinate their

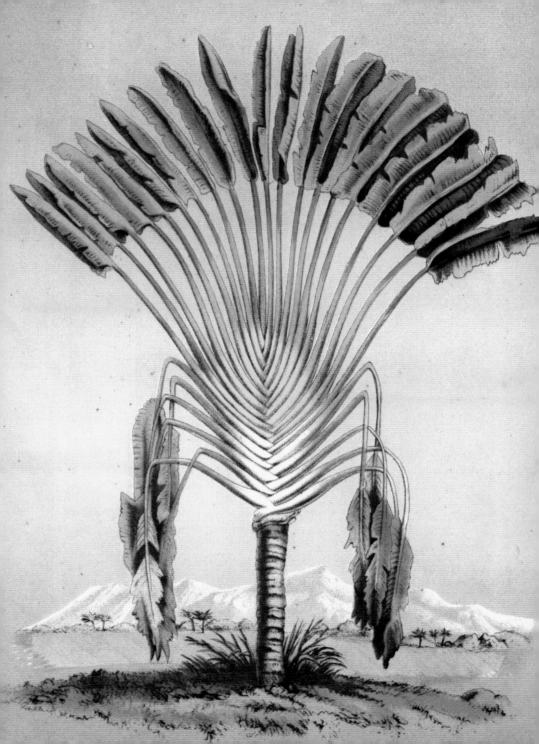

big flowers. The monkeys go to sleep at night, but the flowers work the night shift as well, using other mammals as pollinators, including kinkajous and olingos, both of which are relatives of raccoons.

Madagascar is home to many plants and animals that are found nowhere else, the most famous of them being the lemurs, of which there are around one hundred living or extinct species. But Madagascar also has unique plants, some of them very strange and none, surely, weirder than the traveller's palm, with its huge, long, narrow leaves on long stalks, all held in a plane, like a fan. The plane of the fan tends to be aligned east and west, so its orientation might be of use to a traveller who's lost her compass provided, of course, that she knows which direction is east and which west. Anyway, that's how it acquired its name. Also, the sheaths that enclose the bases of its stalks trap rainwater that might be useful to a traveller – but only a desperately thirsty one, as it's pretty foul.

LEFT: The extraordinary traveller's palm (*Ravenala madagascariensis*), native to Madagascar, is not a true palm. RIGHT: Many animals pollinate flowers. The black-and-white ruffed lemur (*Varecia variegata*) pollinates the traveller's palm.

The traveller's palm is not really a palm tree, but a relative of the bird-of-paradise plants. It bears big white flowers which are pollinated by the ruffed lemur, an attractive black and white primate up to one metre long, not counting the tail. It leaps around confidently high up in the trees, its long muzzle allowing it to reach deep into the flowers. Some have suggested the flowers and lemurs evolved together; at all events, the partnership clearly works for both of them.

Orchid-flowers are not orchids, despite their name. They are eleven species of plants found in tropical southern Asia, one of which in Sarawak, Borneo, produces bilaterally symmetrical flowers just above ground level. The flowers emit a perfume smelling for all the world like dung, so it's not surprising that dung beetles call by. These hard-working beasties collect dung, which they shape into balls that they roll along until they reach what seems to them a suitable spot. Then they stop and lay their eggs inside the dung that will feed their larvae. It's all very practical and the beetles can smell dung from far away and beetle straight for it. When they reach the orchid-flower they acquire a generous sprinkling of pollen, but alas there's no dung for them or, indeed, any other reward. Just the pong. So they leave disappointed, but they never learn. They keep falling for the con.

Does this sound disgusting? If you think so, you'd better skip the next bit because it gets worse. There's a range of names for the different kinds of pollination, all of them ending in -phily. So entomophily is pollination by insects in general, psychophily is pollination by butterflies, melittophily is pollination by bees, cheiropterophily is pollination by bats, myrmecophily is pollination by ants, and so on. And malacophily is pollination by slugs and snails. A slimy practice, I'm sure you'll agree. These aren't the speediest operators and you'd think that by the time one had collected its load of pollen and transported it to another flower it would all be over, the flowers long since faded and gone. But evidently not, because graceful awlsnails have been caught in the act of pollinating prostrate morning glory flowers. This is a weedy plant that blooms in the rainy season, with flowers that open in the morning and are dead by lunchtime. To be fair, honeybees also pollinate them so the flowers aren't wholly dependent on snails that might not get to them in time.

"Malacophily is pollination by slugs and snails, who are not the speediest operators but in practice are surprisingly efficient."

You'll need patience and a bit of luck to see it happening, but you may not have to travel far to observe snails pollinating flowers. Look for golden saxifrage, a plant that occurs throughout Europe and much of temperate Asia. Farther afield, railroad vine, also called bayhops and beach morning glory, is a creeping plant that grows along tropical beaches, colonizing sand dunes. Another morning glory with flowers that last only half a day, it, too, is pollinated by snails, and also by bees. Slugs and snails also pollinate certain duckweeds as they crawl across weed-blanketed ponds.

And the gecko isn't the only lizard pollinator. The mulungu tree, which grows in Brazil, flowers during the dry season and every day its flowers secrete large quantities of nectar that accumulate in the flower bases. The Noronha skink, which is a type of lizard, climbs the trees to lap up the nectar and pollinates the flowers as it does so. Lizard pollinators seem especially common on islands, perhaps because there are fewer mammals and birds.

To the best of my knowledge no plant is pollinated by polar bears. But I live in hope.

Why bother with sex?

—

We can agree, I think, that many flowers really are quite pretty, but can we continue forever to ignore the public displays of indecency that they represent? Is prettiness justification enough for such assaults on our moral sensitivities?

And so to the hard question, which is this: Why bother? Why bother with sexual reproduction at all when there appears to be a perfectly satisfactory alternative? Sex, you see, simply isn't necessary. Lots of organisms, including most plants, are able to manage perfectly well without it.

Consider a humble bacterium. It lives for only twenty minutes or so and then it divides itself in two, so there are two identical copies. After a further twenty minutes each of the copies, or daughters, divides again. So now there are four. And so it continues. Our humble bacterium doubles in number three times an hour. If there was one at noon, by four o'clock there will be 4096 of them. In dying it achieves immortality, not to mention overcrowding. Why would it bother to have male and female genders and go racing around, tiring itself out, searching for partners? A marriage 'til death us do part loses a bit of its lustre when the longest it's likely to last is twenty minutes. There's not even time for the reception.

Then there's the potato. When you buy a bag of seed potatoes they're not actually seeds, you will observe. They're potato tubers that have been grown especially to be planted, and when you put them in the earth you hope that each potato will grow into a new plant, bearing more potatoes. Each of the

The potato (*Solanum tuberosum*) on the left of this illustration produces flowers and seeds like most plants, but it also grows from its tubers, so all the plants that grow from the tubers of this example are genetically identical. Jimsonweed or thorn apple (*Datura stramonium*), on the right, reproduces sexually and is pollinated by nocturnal moths.

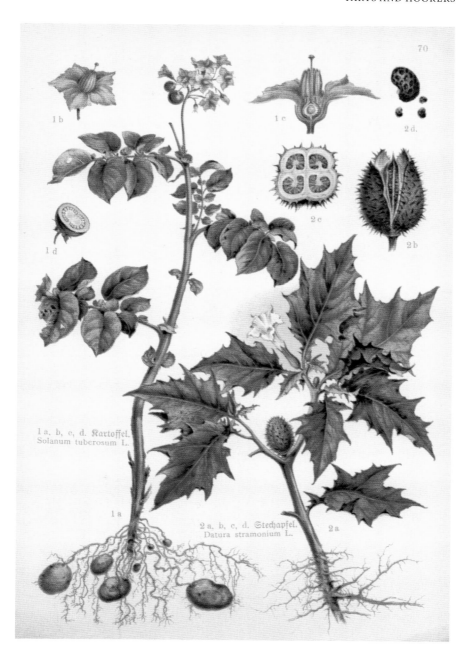

70

1 b

1 c

2 d.

2 c

2 b

1 d

1 a, b, c, d. Kartoffel.
Solanum tuberosum L.

1 a

2 a, b, c, d. Stechapfel.
Datura stramonium L.

2 a

potatoes you harvest will be genetically identical to the tuber you planted. You've gained new plants and tubers without sowing seeds, and sexual reproduction wasn't involved.

Think of what happens when you take a cutting from a plant, tend it until it produces roots and then bed it into the soil so that it grows into a new plant. But is it in fact a new plant? Or is it an extension of the original one? Again, it's genetically identical to the plant you took it from and there's been no sexual reproduction. If you wished, over a few years you could take cutting after cutting and fill your entire garden with what is really a single plant, but one that exists in many copies.

Now, you might be tempted to think that bacteria and garden plants aren't good examples of non-sexual reproduction, that they prove nothing. Bacteria are tiny (but what does that have to do with anything?) and they're simple beings that haven't managed to discover sex. And while farmers and gardeners are able to reproduce plants asexually, that's not what plants choose to do when left to their own devices.

The truth is, though, that bacteria are very far from simple and their behaviour can be highly sophisticated; most plants can reproduce vegetatively, that is to say asexually, by themselves, and many do. In northern Europe, where broad-leaved trees are close to the climatic limit of their range, many species have difficulty in producing seed reliably, year on year, so most of them rely on vegetative reproduction. When you come across a grove of trees of a particular species there's a good chance that all of them are stems of a single tree. As a reproductive strategy, this works very well indeed.

In the Fishlake National Forest, Utah, there's a group of quaking aspens (*Populus tremuloides*) that covers 43 hectares (116 acres) and contains approximately 47,000 apparently individual trees. Only they're not really individuals. Every one of them has descended from shoots arising from nodes on the roots of a single, original tree that died long ago, and as each new stem spread its own roots, more stems arose from them. Genetically identical, they all comprise a single tree and below ground their roots are linked. They call this amazing tree Pando, which is Latin for 'I spread'. Individual stems live for up to about 150 years, but some of the roots are about 80,000 years old and because roots have also died and disappeared the clone as a whole is likely to be much older than that.

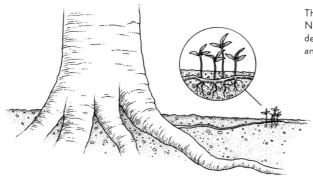

The quaking aspens in Fishlake National Forest, Utah are all descended from a single tree and are genetically identical.

Creosote bushes (*Larrea tridentata*), which live in the Mojave Desert, also clone themselves, but in a different way. When a bush grows old its crown divides into several separate crowns and once this has happened the old crown dies and disappears, leaving each of the daughter crowns to become a separate plant. One such clone, called the King Clone, is believed to be 11,700 years old.

Bracken (*Pteridium aquilinum*), one of the world's most widespread ferns, produces millions of minute spores that are distributed by the wind to germinate into new plants wherever they land in a hospitable spot. This is true of all ferns, but it's quite rare for bracken spores to germinate as the plant's one weakness is that it can't tolerate shade. Consequently, germination is most successful where there has been a fire. Once the plant starts to grow it produces an underground stem called a rhizome, which grows horizontally deep below the surface. Nodes on the deep rhizome give rise to shallow rhizomes and the shallow rhizomes produce leaves that grow upward as the visible ferns to perform the photosynthesis that supplies the plant with food. So a patch of bracken is all one plant. Sections of the deep rhizome eventually die and this may break up the patch into separate groups, but all of them remain genetically identical, all still the same plant. Scientists in Finland have found a patch 450 metres (490 yards) across that's believed to be about 1455 years old.

I've said enough to demonstrate that asexual reproduction clearly works, at least for plants and bacteria. What's more, for plants vegetative reproduction avoids the need to devote all that energy to producing flowers with male and female organs, then finding some way to transfer pollen from male to female individuals. When you've done all that, since sexual reproduction involves the fusion of male and female, you're still only transmitting half of your genes to your offspring. Put this way, sex appears to be grotesquely inefficient. And there's more. If you reproduce asexually you don't need males. It's a thought I find troubling.

So, if sex is unnecessary and costly, why does it exist? Why is it that bacteria, despite being asexual, frequently exchange genes through a tube that one cell extends through the wall of another? The process is called conjugation and the cells able to do it comprise mating types. It's not sex, but it's rather like it. And although most plants are able to reproduce asexually, every so often they grow from seed.

And the answer to my question? No one really knows, but there's at least one plausible suggestion, and the clue is in the bacteria. Biologists know a lot about the history of bacteria. They've found fossil traces of them going back billions of years and the striking thing is that, as far as anyone can tell, bacteria have hardly changed over all that time. It's as though evolution has passed them by. Compare this with flowering plants, which probably didn't exist at all 170 million years ago, but now grow almost everywhere on the planet and have diverged into an estimated 352,000 species.

Each time a bacterium divides it has to make two copies of its DNA, one copy for each daughter. If, during its twenty minutes of fame, that bacterial DNA has been damaged, say by radiation or by some reactive chemical that has entered the cell, both copies will carry that damage, or mutation. Most mutations are harmful and the likely consequence of such damage is that neither of the daughter cells functions correctly. They, or their own daughters, fail to reproduce and the line dies out, taking the mutated DNA with it. There is no way to separate harmful mutations from the very rare mutations that confer an advantage on the cell carrying it, and it is through the accumulation of beneficial mutations that organisms evolve. The result is that it's almost impossible for bacteria to evolve, which is why they've changed so little.

Reproduce sexually, on the other hand, and two sets of DNA are involved. These merge, and during the process harmful and beneficial mutations can be separated. The former tend to be eliminated, while the latter can be acquired from either parent or both, an opportunity that's repeated with each generation. To put this another way, natural selection acts to eliminate harmful mutations and select for beneficial mutations, but in organisms that reproduce asexually, selection acts on the whole organism, whereas in sexually reproducing organisms it acts only upon particular traits.

Establishing new beneficial traits in a population is still a slow and chancy business, but as they spread into the population they combine with the other beneficial traits that preceded them. Once established, the advantages they confer allow the population to increase in size, and the bigger the population the greater the chance of new beneficial mutations occurring and becoming established in their turn. Meanwhile, the elimination of harmful traits is fairly efficient. Sexual reproduction accelerates the rate of evolution, and a fast rate of evolution increases the chance of adapting successfully to changes in the world around us.

Those changes include invasion by organisms that cause diseases and improved efficiency in predators. If they're to survive as disease organisms develop new ways to break into cells, the host cells must constantly upgrade their defences to make their walls impregnable. Plants produce poisons to deter herbivores and as the herbivores acquire tolerance to them, so the plants must make their poisons more potent. It's an arms race. Evolutionary biologists call it the Red Queen effect, from Lewis Carroll's *Alice Through the Looking Glass*, in which the Red Queen said: 'Now *here*, you see, it takes all the running you can do, to keep in the same place. If you want to get somewhere else, you must run at least twice as fast as that.'

Compare this with the fate of the asexual reproducers. Among them, a beneficial mutation will confer its advantage only on the direct descendants of the individual that acquires it. That advantage might allow its possessors to prosper, but even if the trait came to be exchanged between unrelated individuals it would take an extremely long time for it to spread through a population. Harmful mutations, which are much more frequent, also pass to the daughters at each division and they accumulate until they either eliminate entire lines of descendants or seriously impede them. Natural selection might then favour lines of descent with the lowest mutation rate. Evolution must proceed very slowly, and that's why modern bacteria are so similar to their remote ancestors. If sex hadn't been invented, bacteria might have been as far as evolution went. There'd be nothing but bacteria.

"If sex hadn't been invented, bacteria might have been as far as evolution went."

So whom do we have to thank for inventing sex? It's speculation again, but the first sex fiends must have lived in the oceans. Bacteria were fine, but a few of those beneficial mutations resulted in other cells that decided the bacteria were lunch. So the world divided into hunter and hunted and as cells engulfed other cells, now and then the engulfed cells survived inside the cells that had engulfed them. Such cells were more complex than bacteria and in time they began joining together, some to become multicellular plants and others to become plant-eaters.

It's more difficult for a multicelled organism to reproduce simply by dividing in two. It's not impossible. Coral polyps and their relatives can do it, as well as sponges and some roundworms (nematodes), growing a new individual as a bud that breaks away, swimming off to seek its own fortune. But others followed a different route, releasing packets of their DNA into the water. Some packets were capable of dividing to produce new individuals, but only if they were stimulated to do so by packets of a different type. When the two types met they stuck together and began to divide, merging their two sets of DNA as they did so. That was the probable beginning of eggs and sperm and to this day many single-celled aquatic plants and animals reproduce in this way. Once plants moved on to land, and the plant-eating animals and carnivores followed, they continued to release their eggs and sperm into water. Frogs, toads, and newts still do, of course, as do plants such as mosses and liverworts, but vast continents extended beyond the coasts and riverbanks, with fertile soils awaiting colonization. The plants moved into drier regions, the animals faithfully (and hungrily) following, and as they sought to conquer their new worlds they had to devise ways of ensuring productive encounters between sperm and eggs away from water. And, necessity being the mother of invention, they invented sex, clever things. The rest, as they say, is history.

We're forced to conclude that, on the whole, sex brings advantages. Sexual reproduction beats asexual reproduction on several levels. Plants, however, enjoy the best of both worlds. They reproduce sexually, thereby benefiting from accelerated evolution and faster adaptation, but many of them can also reproduce vegetatively.

What is a dandelion?
—

Lion's tooth! *Dent de lion*! Dramatic, isn't it? Say the French version fast enough and the phrase will come to sound more and more like 'dandelion', which is what the name means, referring to the sharply toothed leaf edges which presumably once reminded someone of a lion's teeth. Not being intimately familiar with leonine orthodontics, I can't comment on the accuracy of the name.

The dandelion is the one flower everybody can recognize because it grows pretty well everywhere. If you don't notice the plant itself, or its bright flowers, you can hardly miss its seeds, floating through the air on a sphere of white hairs, the dandelion clocks we all blow away to determine the time of day when we are children. A single dandelion plant may produce more than one thousand clocks a year. Dandelions survive both the mower and the assiduous weeder. The word 'successful' doesn't begin to do them justice.

In addition to their imagined resemblance to teeth, dandelions have many common names, of which wet-a-bed, pissabed, fairy clock, blow ball, monk's head, Irish daisy, priest's crown, and doonheadclock are just a few. Wet-a-bed, pissabed, and the French equivalent piss-en-lit, refer to the strongly diuretic properties of the plant's taproot. But whatever you call them, how have they managed to do so well? It's all down to their love lives, which are strange (to us at least) and have curious consequences.

The dandelion (*Taraxacum* agg.) turns up everywhere and is one of the commonest of all plants – in fact the genus is an aggregate of hundreds of microspecies.

Compositae.

Taraxacum officinale Web.

The most interesting result of the pissabed's sexual proclivities is that it has long ceased to be a proper species at all. Scientists like to name things to bring order to the world, to arrange everything so it can be filed where everybody knows where to find it and what to expect of it. Lion's teeth belong to the aster family, on that there's no disagreement, and the plants comprise the genus *Taraxacum*, again by common consent. But beyond that, chaos sets in. There are an estimated 235 or so *Taraxacum* species in Britain alone, and I doubt anyone can even guess how many there are worldwide. Figures of five hundred or even two thousand have been quoted. The differences are small, so they're known as microspecies, and although the dandelion used to be called *Taraxacum officinale*, nowadays the reference books simply list *Taraxacum* agg., for aggregate. It's the best anyone can do. And to complicate matters further, there are other related wild plants, such as catsears and hawkweeds, which look very like dandelions. The aster family is especially good at producing species with yellow composite flowers.

So next time you stare balefully at the dandelion that's cheerfully and cheekily opening its flower between the slabs of your patio or in the middle of the lawn you mowed yesterday, try treating it with a bit more respect. There's no doubt it's a dandelion, but can you tell which one? Now, I bet that will have you stumped. Here's a clue. Such differences between microspecies as are visible show up in the leaves, not the flowers. So compare the numbers and arrangements of the teeth against leaves from different dandelion plants. That will tell you whether the plants you sample belong to different microspecies, but putting a name to those microspecies is a job not simply for a botanist, but for a botanist who specializes in dandelions.

At first sight, a dandelion flower looks much like other flowers. It's a type of aster, so the flower is a composite, but in this case one that consists only of hundreds of ray florets, with no central disc florets. If you rub the flower on someone's face it will make a yellow mark. That's pollen. Ants, bees, and butterflies visit the flower. When I was a small boy and wondered whether dandelions had a smell I sniffed one to find out, and ants ran all over my face. The flower is followed by the seeds that allow us to tell the time and, when they've done that, to germinate and grow into more dandelions. So far, so ordinary. But that's only one side of the story.

As you know, when plants or animals reproduce sexually, genes from both parents combine. But the dandelion is one of a number of plants in which a female egg cell is able to multiply until it forms a seed that's capable of germinating to produce a new plant. The tiny seed, at the centre of its clock, is different from other seeds in only one respect. It carries the genes only of its mother. This trick is called apomixis or, to be absolutely precise, a variety of apomixis called agamospermy, which means apomixis by seeds. It's parthenogenesis, of course, which is the posh name for virgin birth.

The significance of apomixis is that all the new young dandelion plants that spring up wherever the seeds fall are clones, and genetically identical to each other and to their single mum. Each new plant produces seeds apomictically, becoming a single mum herself, and her fairy clocks float away on the wind to become single mums in their turn.

Remember, though, that each time a cell divides there's a risk of a copying mistake and over time exposure to a variety of environmental hazards can cause genes to mutate. Errors don't occur every time, obviously, but occasionally one does and very occasionally the mistake, or mutation, is either beneficial or at least neutral, in that it may confer no advantage but neither does it do any harm. So the difference survives and descendants of that plant inherit it. Over many generations the accumulated alterations render that line of descendants subtly different from all the others. Only there's not simply one line of descendants, of course – there are many, and as time passes the differences between them increase. Genetically, the lines gently, slowly, drift apart. The differences have only minor influences on the plants' appearance, but they may be sufficient to prevent members of one line of descent from mating successfully with members of another line, assuming they might wish to do so. When that happens, the two lines have become two species, or in the case of the dandelions, in which the process has not gone that far, microspecies. It's no wonder, then, that there are so many microspecies and that biologists find it impossible to classify them in neat groups.

So the dandelions have escaped the constraints of sex, but there are dangers in doing that. Sooner or later accumulated deleterious mutations may wipe out entire lines of descent. But the dandelions are too canny to be caught by that one. Some of them reproduce sexually. They produce regular pollen that insects transfer to regular stigmas, to fertilize regular ovules and produce regular seeds – seeds, that is, with a dad as well as a mum. These regular seeds look no different as they float away in their clocks.

You think this is complicated? Just wait. As well as dandelions that reproduce sexually and dandelions that reproduce asexually, certain apomictic clones can reproduce sexually and there are two types of sexual reproducers. A study of a population of Dutch dandelions found that about one-third reproduced sexually, two-thirds asexually, and fewer than one per cent of the plants belonged to the alternative sexual group. What happens is that some pollen from apomictic plants is capable of fertilizing sexually reproducing plants and this leads to a cycle of sexual and asexual reproduction throughout the population, and plants resulting from sexual reproduction are capable of apomixis. It's win-win for the dandelions. They gain the advantages of rapid, low-cost, asexual reproduction, while allowing sufficient mixing of genes to avoid the dangers of excessive inbreeding.

So much for exotic mating habits, but dandelions are belt-and-braces plants. Cut a dandelion taproot into bits and each bit can produce a new plant. Not to put too fine a point on it, they're also happy to reproduce vegetatively whenever an enthusiastic gardener offers them the opportunity.

Their reproductive behaviour also explains why you often find crowds of dandelions all growing close together. The combination of apomixis, sexual reproduction, and vegetative reproduction tends to favour dense stands, each stand being a clone of genetically identical individuals.

All of this answers another question for gardeners. The dandelions have reproduction down to a fine art and they're nothing if not versatile. There's no way you'll defeat them, so you may as well learn to love them. They have medicinal properties, all parts are edible (if you're not too fussy), you can brew a country wine from the flowers, and the white latex that exudes from their broken stems has been talked of as a source of natural rubber. Only it seems to me you'd need an awful lot of dandelions to make a bike tyre.

They're not even bad news as weeds. Their taproots absorb nutrients from the soil below the level most of their neighbours can reach and bring them up to the stem, leaves, and flower. When these parts of the plant die down their decomposition releases the nutrients near the soil surface, where all the other plants can reach them. So dandelions may be weeds, but they're beneficial weeds. Since you can't win anyway, maybe it would be best to leave them alone to get on with it – they are a cheery sight.

You might wonder what it is that makes dandelions so much smarter than other plants. If their method of no-sex reproduction is such a great idea, why haven't other plants taken it up? What's so special about dandelions? That's simple: nothing. There are more than three hundred species of plants that reproduce apomictically. They include wild relatives of maize, wheat and pearl millet; several other grasses, including various meadow grasses; and hawkweeds, lady's mantle, agave, rowans, whitebeams and some hawthorns. Some onions also reproduce this way, including Chinese chive. In fact, well over half of all the plant species growing wild in Britain reproduce apomictically.

Apart from dandelions, the most familiar plant to reproduce this way is also another of the most troublesome when it finds its way into your shrubbery – the common bramble. Harvesting blackberries along the hedgerows is a traditional late summer pastime. You can still see whole families out on Sunday afternoons with their pots and jars and plastic bags, hands stained, wrists scratched, children fed up, gathering the basic ingredient for jams and jellies and home-made booze.

Have you ever wondered why blackberries gathered from different hedgerows often look and taste different? Is one hedgerow more exposed to the sunshine than another, or is the soil richer, or is there more shelter from winds and late frosts? Such factors may well play a part, but the most likely explanation is that the brambles themselves are different microspecies, end-products of lines of asexual descent. In Europe alone there are 748 species of bramble, of which 744 are apomicts. No wonder brambles are so successful, and offer so much variety. And, of course, they're cultivated commercially too.

Rural hedgerows and suburban lawns aren't especially hostile places to put down roots if you're a plant, so a plant that reproduces as efficiently as dandelions and brambles is bound to flourish. And an unchosen plant that flourishes soon becomes regarded as an invasive weed, doomed to pointless persecution no matter how nutritious, tasty or therapeutic it may be. Gardens and hedgerows aren't really the places where this reproductive stratagem comes into its own. To find that you need to look in places where life is hard for any plant.

Apomicts colonize disturbed ground, where their ability to multiply rapidly allows them to establish themselves ahead of their more conventionally sexual rivals. They also prosper where the growing season is short and pollinators scarce, for example in alpine and arctic habitats. Perhaps surprisingly, they appear in tropical forests, too. That's because a tropical forest is likely to be crowded with such a diversity of species that cross-breeding can be difficult, since individuals of a particular species are at risk of becoming separated by barriers formed from plants of other species. Apomixis solves the problem for individuals isolated in this, or any other, way.

Glaciers can also cut through landscapes, dividing them into discrete areas separated by ice barriers that seeds and pollinators cannot easily cross. Such carving up of the countryside also favours the establishment of apomictic species that are no longer able to exchange genes with former partners on the other side.

Such reproductive talent has obvious potential, and plant breeders, always on the lookout for ways to improve crop plants, have been studying apomixis for years. Think of the advantages if cereal and fruit crops no longer had to rely on pollination, especially by unreliable wind or by the complicated procedures used to pollinate maize. They're experimenting with apomictic maize and also with forage grasses. One day, perhaps soon, we'll be less reliant on the insect pollinators. Sex will be less important, at least for plants.

CHAPTER 3

THE
SHY ONES
AND THE
NARCISSISTS

———

A journey into the intimate world of open
and closed marriages, 'selfers' and a plant
with seven genders – oh my.

Shrinking violets

—

Shyness can be a dreadful affliction that in severe cases drives people to avoid social contact altogether. To a shy person it seems preferable to stay away from others, avoiding social gatherings and especially parties, rather than suffer the stress of trying to talk to strangers or join in with activities others seem to find enjoyable but to the shy person appear pointless, difficult, and embarrassing. So shy people hide away, retreat to shady corners where they won't be noticed, or find excuses for being absent. They acquire the reputation of being shrinking violets.

So who was Violet and what made her shrink? Well, she wasn't a person at all, but a flower, and it's the nineteenth-century writer and poet Leigh Hunt who is credited with having first described a violet as 'shrinking', originally by comparison with buttercups. Violets really do shrink, too, as a way of dealing with problems caused by plants much bigger than they are, the ones you might think of as the show-offs and bullies.

There are up to 600 species of violets. Most are found in temperate regions of the northern hemisphere, but a small number occur more widely. A few are shrubs but most are small herbs, and the group includes the pansies. The garden pansy, a popular bedding plant that fills municipal borders and the tills at garden centres, is a hybrid, one of its ancestors being the wild pansy. Garden pansies and cultivated violets don't shrink. The Parks Department wouldn't put up with it. Shrinking has been bred out of them and anyway they don't need it. As you can see when you're confronted by acres of them, they're anything but shy. Indeed, I'd be tempted to call them brazen hussies.

The common or dog violet (*Viola riviniana*), one of up to 600 species of *Viola*, has flowers that really do shrink. It is the most widespread violet.

VIOLA RIVINIANA RCHB. 1283.

Like most familiar wild flowers the wild pansy has a long list of names, including tickle-my-fancy, come-and-cuddle-me, jack-jump-up-and-kiss-me, and love-in-idleness. Need I say more?

The wild pansy may possess remarkable powers. You'll recall that in *A Midsummer Night's Dream* Oberon, king of the fairies, seeking to punish Titania, his queen with whom he has quarrelled over a stolen human infant they both claim, explains to Puck the weapon he will use.

> 'That very time I saw, — but thou couldst not, —
> Flying between the cold moon and the earth,
> Cupid all arm'd: a certain aim he took
> At a fair vestal, throned by the west;
> And loos'd his love-shaft smartly from his bow,
> As it should pierce a hundred thousand hearts;
> But I might see young Cupid's fiery shaft
> Quench'd in the chaste beams of the watery moon:
> And the imperial votaress passed on,
> In maiden meditation, fancy-free.
> Yet mark'd I where the bolt of Cupid fell:
> It fell upon a little western flower, —
> Before milk-white, now purple with love's wound, —
> And maidens call it love-in-idleness.
> Fetch me that flower; the herb I show'd thee once;
> The juice of it on sleeping eyelids laid
> Will make or man or woman madly dote
> Upon the next live creature that it sees.
> Fetch me this herb: and be thou here again
> Ere the leviathan can swim a league.'
>
> (Act II, Sc. II)

And when Puck returns with the flower, Oberon tells him where he will find Titania sleeping, again among the violets:

> 'I know a bank whereon the wild thyme blows,
> Where ox-lips and the nodding violet grows;
> Quite over-canopied with lush woodbine,
> With sweet musk roses, and with eglantine:
> There sleeps Titania sometime of the night ...'

I confess I've never tried this love potion myself so I don't know whether it works, and in any case I'm not Oberon and that probably makes a difference. And while we're on the subject, I don't know how to change someone's head into the head of an ass, either.

Going back to the botany, wild violets and pansies are woodland plants. You'll find them growing in shaded places around forest clearings and on roadside verges, but also in flower meadows. They're small, no more than twelve centimetres (five inches) tall and with flowers much smaller than those of the blowsy cultivated varieties. The sweet violet (*Viola odorata*) is fragrant and people have been wearing its perfume since the days of ancient Greece. Victorian ladies were particularly taken with it.

Violet flowers are bilaterally symmetrical, indicating that insects pollinate them. When you meet violets in their natural surroundings, it's clear why Leigh Hunt described them as shrinking. They sit there demurely, hugging the ground, smaller than most of the flowers around them. You might think they're crouching timidly, a bit embarrassed, hoping you won't notice them and, if you do, that you won't try to engage them in a conversation or ask them to do anything they'd find challenging. They'd blush if they knew how to.

That's one sense in which violets might be thought to be shrinking, but it's not very convincing, is it? There are plenty of other small, low-growing plants, after all, with small flowers. What about scarlet pimpernels, up to fourteen millimetres (about half an inch) across, or eyebright with flowers up to ten

PLANT LOVE

millimetres (a third of an inch) across? They're tiny, but no one
describes them as shrinking.

Clearly there must be more to it, and there is. It has to do
with the way the violet flowers work. In early spring the flowers
open in the ordinary way. These are the flowers you see on the
verges and in the woodlands. They have five petals, five sepals,
and five stamens, and insects pollinate them. Once fertilized,
the flowers produce fruit capsules filled with seeds. The
capsules dry, and when drying has shrunk them by a certain
amount they explode, hurling out their cargoes of seeds,
some of them flying several metres. The seeds germinate,
and round we go.

There's one odd thing, though. Some of these highly visible
flowers are sterile. The common blue violet, which grows in
eastern North America, is one of them. But in most species the
flowers reproduce in the usual way.

Then, in late summer or autumn, the plants flower for a
second time, and this time they're truly shrinking. The flowers
have no petals, so there's no bright splash of colour, and the
sepals never open, so there's no very obvious change in the
appearance of the flower buds. But the flowers are fully active.
Each flower fertilizes itself, on the inside as it were, so there's
nothing to see until the sepals fall away from the fruit capsules,
which dry in the usual way and burst to eject the year's second
batch of seeds. Again there are exceptions. The birdfoot violet
(*V. pedata*) of North America cannot pollinate itself and relies
on bees.

Why have they evolved to do this? The second flowering
is a form of insurance. Just in case the pollinators unkindly
passed the spring flowers by, or fertilization failed for some
other reason, a summer or autumn flowering gives the plant a
second chance at reproducing. The problem, however, is that
by summer all the other plants are leaping up aggressively
all over the place, waving their big leaves and huge flowers
about high above the ground in that dreadfully blatant way
they have, and the wee violets and pansies don't have much
hope of attracting a pollinator. They're just too hard to see for

98

insects dodging this way and that as they weave through the vegetation. It's a case of the one that shouts the loudest gets the attention. Whispering gets you nowhere. So the violets, which sense the shade cast by the bigger plants all around them, don't even attempt to compete with all the noise and bustle that's going on. They become introspective, remain firmly closed, fertilize themselves, and in due course chuck out their seeds, job done. If the insects can't be bothered, well, that's their loss. What's more, the plants don't have to go to all the trouble and expense of producing petals. The flowers are shrinking all right, but shrinking with a purpose, and it works. It's inbreeding, of course, but that doesn't matter because most of them produce outbreeding flowers in spring, which is enough to keep the genes mixing.

Self-fertilization without the flower opening is called cleistogamy, for those who like to keep up with the botanical jargon. The name means 'closed marriage', and it's contrasted with fertilization with open flowers, called chasmogamy, or 'open marriage'. And as you know, closed marriages are morally much superior to open marriages, which usually end in tears all over the gossip columns.

If a reproductive stratagem works, you'd expect it to be fairly common, and so it is. Violets are by no means the only ones to alternate chasmogamy with cleistogamy. The world's full of part-time moral plants, the shrinkers.

Jewelweed (*Impatiens capensis*) is one. Also called orange balsam, spotted touch-me-not and several other names, it's a widely cultivated native of North America that has escaped and established itself in the wild in Britain, often growing beside ditches and along riverbanks. The name jewelweed may refer to the way its leaves appear silver under water, and it's called touch-me-not because its seed capsules explode if they're touched, even lightly. Its flowers are big and rich in nectar. Bees seek them out.

Jewelweeds resort to cleistogamy when they find themselves in stable but mildly inhospitable environments. As

264

Gr.Bufoniu erectum ~~~~ *angustifolium maius.*

V. 2.

Toad rush (*Juncus bufonius*) grows in damp places throughout
the temperate northern hemisphere. It's another plant that
produces seeds without ever opening its flowers.

with the violets, it's a kind of reproductive insurance, but in this case scientists have found there's a bit more to it. Fewer ovules are fertilized in self-fertilizing closed flowers than in open flowers, but fertilization is most successful in the open flowers produced by plants that grow from self-fertilized seeds. This suggests that the plants have evolved a way to reduce the harm arising from inbreeding.

Wood sorrel, *Oxalis acetosella*, is another spring-flowering woodland herb. It's sometimes called alleluia because its pale, delicate flowers usually open around Eastertime. It opens its petals by day and closes them at night; a demure plant, you might say, with respectable habits. Well, that's the impression it likes to give. We all know people like that. The reality is somewhat more practical.

Flowering at Easter means cutting a few corners. Wood sorrel is a perennial and evergreen, so it's primed and ready to start growing the instant the sunshine shows signs of strengthening, the nights grow shorter, and the soil starts to warm. But then it has to grow fast. It's a small plant, only up to ten centimetres (four inches) tall. Its roots are fragile and its flower petals are very thin, because there's no time to make them stronger. That's why it closes its flowers, at night when the pollinators aren't flying, but sometimes also during the day to protect them from strong sunshine or rain, or when it is touched. It all pays off, because the wood sorrel is able to open its flowers while the other plants are still getting started, and the flowers are easy for the early insects to find because there are few others around. In late summer, wood sorrel flowers for a second time, but this time without petals and without opening its flower buds, just like the violet.

Toad rush (*Juncus bufonius*) is another cleistogam. It's an annual plant, resembling a slender grass and up to twenty centimetres (eight inches) tall, that grows in damp places throughout temperate regions of the northern hemisphere. Linnaeus named it, calling it bufonius (toad) because it grows in the sort of damp places where you find toads. Gardeners tend to consider it a weed. It flowers from May to September, but without the flowers opening. Its fruits are capsules that break open to release up to about one hundred seeds each, so a single plant may produce more than 30,000 seeds in a year.

Some plants practise self-fertilization inside closed flowers when faced with competition from close relatives. Consider the deadnettles, in particular red deadnettle, also called purple deadnettle or purple archangel (*Lamium purpureum*) and henbit deadnettle, also called greater henbit (*L. amplexicaule*). Both are annual herbs growing to about twenty centimetres (eight inches) tall, and they're very similar in appearance. As you see, they both belong to the same genus, *Lamium*, which means they're close relatives. They grow on bare ground, often forming quite dense stands, and gardeners regard them as weeds, though not especially troublesome ones.

A team of Japanese botanists studied a population of both species growing together beside a road on the campus of Kyoto University. They observed that when henbit deadnettle found itself growing close to red deadnettle it produced more closed than open flowers, and the proportion of closed flowers increased the more red deadnettle there was growing nearby. Where the henbit deadnettle grew among its own kind, however, it produced fewer closed flowers, no matter how densely packed the plants were. The scientists went to three other sites where the two plants were growing, in different parts of Japan and far from each other, and they found the same effect. They then transplanted henbit deadnettle plants into a stand of red deadnettle and collected the seeds from both open and closed henbit deadnettle flowers, finding no difference in the number of seeds each type of flower produced.

So if cleistogamy makes no difference to seed production, what is its point? The scientists had no answer. The only clue may lie in the fact that henbit deadnettle grows naturally throughout all but the most northern regions of Japan but red deadnettle was first recorded in Japan in the late nineteenth century and is now naturalized throughout the country.

So despite being close relatives, the two species have been growing side by side for little more than a century. Plants live more slowly than we do, so it's quite possible they've yet to get used to each other and henbit deadnettle fears that the pollinating insects may prefer the incomer. Rather than risk it, it keeps its flowers closed when in proximity to what it considers its rival.

Almost seven hundred species of plants reproduce by cleistogamy, although they are also able to produce open flowers, so the method appears to have evolved many times independently in unrelated plant families. It occurs most often in grasses. Annual fescue and an annual blue grass practise this technique, and so does littleseed muhly, an annual clump-forming grass that grows in dry, scrub areas of southern California. Cleistogamy also occurs in some crop plants. The Sathi variety of rice uses it, as does the West African Nunaba cultivar of sorghum, and it's found in some varieties of wild barley. Rice plants are prone to becoming sterile when they flower at high temperatures, and Japanese researchers have found that when they raised the temperature to trigger cleistogamy, pollination was better in the cleistogamous plants and they produced more seed.

As with so many of the successful strategies plants have developed over the millennia, botanists are reckoning to exploit cleistogamy in new ways. If they can develop genetically modified plants that are cleistogamous, they'll eliminate the risk of pollen from GM plants fertilizing non-GM plants. That will prevent GM genes from escaping into the environment. Cleistogamy may also protect crops against disease caused by fungi that attack the developing seed head.

Secretive Figs and the Underground Orchid

—

You'd surely think, wouldn't you, that the violet and all those other cleistogamous plants had taken the business of shrinking about as far as it ought to go. I mean to say, having flowers that are designed never to open, lack both petals and perfume and produce fruits which suddenly appear as if from nowhere and explode their seeds all over the place – that isn't going to impress the garden centre manager, is it? But, believe it or not, some plants have gone even further. One of the most remarkable is the fig.

There are something like 850 species of figs. They're woody plants that grow as trees, shrubs, vines, and as epiphytes, which are plants that grow on the surface of other plants. Figs occur throughout the tropics and most have fruit that's edible. The fig you buy in the supermarket, fresh or dried, is the fruit of the common fig (*Ficus carica*). It's a little different from other figs in that it grows naturally in more temperate climes, including the Mediterranean region, and gardeners grow it as far north as Britain. That's the only fig that's been widely cultivated as a source of food, although a number of other species are grown in parts of Asia for local consumption.

When you buy a box of dried figs for Christmas or a summer punnet of fresh ones you probably think you're buying a perfectly ordinary fruit. And probably that's what the retailer wants you to believe. Misleading you is a lot easier than explaining that in fact the fig is a false fruit – though apples and pears are also false fruits too, if it comes to it, and nobody in the shop bothers to explain them, either.

Slice your fig in half and you find it's full of seeds embedded in a sweet-tasting kind of fibrous pulp. There may be hundreds of seeds or even thousands. Seeds, as you know, are what you get from fertilized flowers, but you can stare at a fig tree till the cows come home and you won't see any flowers, not even a tiny one you'd barely notice hiding behind a leaf. What you will see, if you're lucky, is figs. They start out small and as the season advances they grow bigger until, if the weather's favourable, they ripen and you can pick and eat them. They're very nutritious, full of vitamins and sugar. But there's never a flower in sight.

A standard sort of flower, you'll recall, rests upon a base called the receptacle. All its male and female organs grow from the receptacle. In the case of the fig, the outer part of the structure, the 'skin' you hold in your fingers, is the receptacle and, as you can see, it has curled over and completely closed itself, so that on the tree it grows outward from the axil where a leaf stalk branches from the main stem, at the end of a flower stalk, a peduncle. And since that's how it develops there's only one place for the flower to be, and that's on the inside. Only there's not just one flower but many, forming an inflorescence. It's an inflorescence composed of florets that open, bloom, and set seed, and those are the seeds you eat when you eat the 'fruit'. It's not a true fruit, though, but a false fruit known as a synconium.

All those florets on the inside are pollinated, pollen being transferred from males to females in the regular way. Some fig species have hermaphrodite flowers and others have a mixture of hermaphrodite and female flowers. Hermaphrodite figs produce synconia called caprifigs that can be fed to livestock, especially goats – *capra* is Latin for goat – but people find them inedible.

Pollination implies a pollinator, so you'll see at once that the fig has a problem, having completely enclosed its flowers. If you look closely at a synconium, however, you may notice a tiny opening, like a pore, near the end farthest from the stalk. That pore is the door by which the pollinators enter. Obviously, the pollinators are tiny. In fact they're female wasps small enough to pass through the eye of an ordinary sewing needle with no difficulty and they're specialized for this way of life. There are approximately 900 species of these wasps and at one time botanists believed each species of fig had its

own pollinator, its own fig wasp, and that wasp never visited any other fig. They know now that they were mistaken; the wasps aren't that choosy and a fig is likely to be visited by several species.

The tight fit as she crawls through the entrance and into the flower-filled wasp paradise pulls off the female's wings and often her antennae as well, but she won't need them again as it's a one-way trip – once she's inside the synconium there's no way out. She's not there to admire the view, it being totally dark, or to selflessly pollinate the figs, of course, but is looking, or rather feeling, for suitable places to lay her eggs. If she's entered a caprifig, the wasp, known as a foundress and you'll see why, will come across female florets with styles that are short enough for her ovipositor to reach all the way to the ovary. She'll move from floret to floret, depositing her load of pollen on the stigmas and laying one or two eggs in each ovary until all her eggs are gone and then, her task done, she dies. If she enters an edible synconium, on the other hand, she'll find the female florets have styles that are too long for her ovipositor to reach the ovary and she'll die without laying. But in searching for a suitable floret she'll crawl across the stigmas of many female florets, depositing on them the pollen she carries from the synconium where she herself hatched.

A gall-like structure forms around the eggs and in due course the first of them hatch, the larvae feeding on the contents of the ovary until they mature into wingless male wasps, which bite holes in the ovary to escape. Each new male escapee crawls to another floret with an ovary containing a female wasp. He chews a hole through the ovary wall and inserts his abdomen to fertilize the female occupant. The female climbs out through the hole he made, then both females and males leave the synconium. As the female wasps crawl across the flowers toward the exit they collect pollen from the

The common fig (*Ficus carica*) is the species most widely cultivated for its false fruits.

male flowers, then leave the synconium to find another fig where they can lay their own eggs and deposit their pollen. It's a tough life and a brief one; they have only forty-eight hours to achieve this before they die, but at least they get a glimpse of the outside world. The males die almost as soon as they emerge, once they've fertilized the females, and their eyes are tiny and rudimentary, so they can't do any glimpsing. Natural selection reckoned they didn't need eyes that work.

From the fig's point of view, it's a cunning arrangement. Wasps can lay eggs only in synconia with short-style florets and they carry pollen from there to synconia with long styles in which the wasps are unable to lay eggs. It guarantees that florets can't fertilize themselves.

But what if some of the wasps cheat? What if a wasp lays her eggs without contributing any pollen? Or what if she's lazy and leaves more than one or two eggs in the ovary? When that happens, and sometimes it does, the plant either kills the floret or allows only a very few wasp eggs to develop. Plants are far from helpless when dealing with criminals.

The synconium produces seed and is now ripe, and it changes colour to advertise the fact. Before long a fig-loving animal chances along, scoffs the fig and goes on its way, at some time later and at some distance voiding the seeds in its nutrient-rich faeces. And the wheel of life makes another turn.

Consider, though, the dilemma facing Alice Figwasp as she flies around the tree choosing her synconium. We should all be wary of one-way entrances to chambers with no exit, and there's a trap for those who aren't. Each foundress is concerned only to find flowers in which to lay her eggs and in doing so she will pollinate only a few florets. If the inflorescence is to be pollinated effectively, therefore, many wasps will be required. That being so, let's return to Alice. What if she were to enter through the tiny door only to find herself at the waspy equivalent of the Mad Hatter's tea party? 'No room, no room,' the wasps would cry, as Alice crawled haplessly from one occupied floret to the next, with no means of admitting her mistake, apologizing for the interruption and leaving quietly. What should a poor wasp do? Well, Alice is no one's fool. As she examines each synconium in turn she notes the piles of discarded wings and antennae around the entrance portal – body parts that were stripped from the wasps now inside laying eggs. So it's simple. A large pile of wings and antennae indicates a crowded inflorescence, so Alice looks for a synconium with no or at best just a few wasp bits and pieces lying on its surface, a sure sign of an abundance of vacant florets.

Now, I'm sure you will have spotted the lack of a fly of sorts in my ointment. If this is what happens, when you slice open a fig you should see at least some wasp corpses and probably a few larvae. Only there's no sign of them.

Absence of evidence, the sleuths will tell you, is not evidence of absence, but it's not as bad as it sounds. Waste not want not: the fig plant secretes an enzyme that digests dead wasps, so most of the wasp remains have gone by the time you get your figs home. But there will be a few remaining, and some larvae. Fear not, for they're too small to see and they can't harm you in any way.

And the fig growers are on your side, for their own reasons, naturally. If too many wasps enter the inflorescence and pollinate florets, so many seeds will develop that the synconium bursts. The explosion scatters the seeds, so the plant is happy, but wrecked fruits aren't so good for the grower's cash flow. To minimize the risk to their bank balances, commercial growers plant trees bearing caprifigs far away from those bearing edible figs, and they control the number of fig wasps by buying bags of them from a supplier and releasing them in a controlled way.

Figs have an importance extending far beyond their role as a food source. The Buddha attained enlightenment while meditating in the shade of a sacred fig, *Ficus religiosa*, and this is also the tree that Hindus revere as the world tree. The banyan, *F. benghalensis*, is India's national tree. It was the fig tree that supplied the leaves with which Adam and Eve preserved their modesty, and fig leaves have been used ever since to cover the genitals of naked folk in paintings and sculptures. During Queen Victoria's reign, male nudity was frowned upon and a fig leaf was cast in plaster and kept at the ready, in case of a visit by the monarch, to cover the genitals of a copy of a statue of David in the Victoria and Albert Museum in London.

Many birds, bats, monkeys and other arboreal animals of the tropical forest feed on figs, greatly helping these plants, which often grow as epiphytes. The fig-eaters, especially birds, deposit seeds high in the crowns of forest trees, where they germinate and can expose their leaves to the bright sunshine. The young fig plants rely on their host tree only for support and produce aerial roots that grow downward from the crown all the way to the forest floor, where they penetrate and anchor themselves, becoming regular roots. As they age, those parts of the roots that are above ground grow thicker until eventually they resemble trunks. The banyans are spectacular examples, with their multiple stem-like roots forming groves that afford shade from the tropical sun.

But there's a dark side. The aerial roots may descend down the trunk of their host tree, in contact with it. As they thicken, the roots contact one another, the bark between them disappears, and the roots merge. Eventually the roots form a continuous woody cover surrounding the host trunk, while at the same time the top of the fig grows upward until its leaves shade those of the host. In time this may kill the host tree, which dies and decomposes, leaving the fig as a free-standing, hollow 'stemmed' tree. It's then known as a strangler fig.

Let's face it, growing flowers that are never meant to be seen is pretty weird. But figs, with their synconia, aren't alone. There's one plant that lives its entire life several centimetres below ground. It bears attractive flower heads – capitula – about three centimetres (one inch) across, with white or cream bracts that form a head resembling a tulip enclosing up to about 150 dark maroon ray and ring florets. Only you'll never see them because the flowers, too, bloom below ground. There's a small opening at the ground surface immediately above the capitulum, covered by bark and leaf litter that hide it.

There's one plant that lives its entire life several centimetres below ground.

The plant is the western underground orchid, and it grows in Western Australia, where a farmer called John Trott discovered it in May 1928, while he was ploughing land that had previously been rolled. He noticed a sweet smell apparently emanating from a curious crack in the ground and found the plant when he explored further. Trott sent the plant to Charles Gardner, the government botanist, who sent it to another botanist, Richard Rogers, who described it. The orchid ended up with Gardner's name, as *Rhizanthella gardneri*. More of these plants were found in subsequent years, always in bushland that was being ploughed after having been burnt and rolled, but it remains so rare that its known locations are closely guarded secrets. So far only about three hundred specimens have been found.

Since it lives below ground, the underground orchid is unable to perform photosynthesis and necessarily lives as a parasite. It obtains nutrients from the broom honey-myrtle, a shrub or small tree that forms thickets, by linking to a fungus that lives in a close relationship with the host plant. Drought and the death of old plants mean that thickets of honey-myrtle are becoming increasingly rare in the wheat-growing area of Australia where they're found, and the orchid is categorized as critically endangered because its habitat is disappearing.

The orchid produces a succulent horizontal rhizome, or subterranean stem, some 6–12 centimetres (2½–5 inches) below the surface, which smells of formalin if you cut through it. The orchid is able to reproduce vegetatively, yielding up to three new plants in this way, but the daughter plants reproduce sexually, with underground insects performing pollinating duties. Termites and fungus gnats are especially useful in this regard.

The plant begins to flower in late May or early June and it takes the fertilized flowers about six months to set fleshy, berry-like fruits, each containing twenty to fifty seeds. This is unusual in itself, in that most orchids produce their seeds in pods. So far as anyone knows, the plants have no mechanism for seed dispersal. What seems to happen is that the mature flowers die and decompose, and it is their decomposition that releases the seeds.

The western underground orchid has one close relative, the eastern underground orchid (*Rhizanthella slateri*), which grows in parts of Queensland and New South Wales and lives on nutrients it acquires from fungi among dead and decaying plant matter. It has a succulent rhizome about fifteen centimetres (six inches) long and in October and November produces capitula about two centimetres (nearly one inch) across comprising up to about thirty florets. It's not quite so reclusive as its western cousin because its purple capitula do penetrate the ground surface, although they remain covered by dead leaves so they're very difficult to find. The insects that pollinate the flowers manage to find them, however, which is what matters to the orchid. Eastern underground orchids grow in eucalyptus forest, but the largest population ever discovered comprised no more than about eight flower heads and the plants have been found at fewer than ten sites. It is at least as endangered as the better-known western species.

The western underground orchid (*Rhizanthella gardneri*),
found in Western Australia, spends its entire life below ground.

Flowers
without petals
—

I've not the slightest doubt that you'll join with me in applauding the exemplary modesty of the figs and underground orchids. Admittedly, the habit some figs have of strangling to death the trees that have given them a good start in life is unfortunate, to say the least, and makes them in that respect unsuited to be botanical role models, but despite that, their insistence on privacy to perform the most private of acts must be highly commended. Would that other plants might show a similar sense of decorum.

Of course, it's not possible for all plants to turn their flowers inside out or bury them below ground. That would be asking too much of plants unaccustomed to such contortions. We must be reasonable. But there's no need to go to such extremes. Modesty may be protected in other ways, and it is perfectly possible to conduct the search for partners or spouses in public, while remaining discreet. There are many plants, including some of the most successful at the game of life, and consequently the most abundant, which perform their courtship and mating dances before our very eyes, yet as it were invisibly. As all spooks and pickpockets know, the best place to achieve invisibility is in full view of everyone.

Consider the catkins that dangle demurely, quivering in the breeze like kittens' tails, which is where the word 'catkin' originated, from the Dutch for kitten, *katteken*. We know spring is coming when the hazel catkins appear, hanging down from their twigs and appearing before the leaves are even thinking of unfurling themselves in the big green stretch of a new year. Hazel isn't the only tree to sport springtime catkins, of course. Alders bear them, as do birches, sweet chestnuts, oaks, hickory, and many more. A catkin is an inflorescence, consisting of a host of minute florets crowded around a central stem. In most cases all the florets are male, and though you and I may think them attractive they're not out to attract us, nor even the insects. And because they have no interest in animals of any sort, they don't bother to produce petals, far less brightly coloured petals. They've no need to be showy.

If the catkins are male flowers, where, I hear you ask, are the females? For surely the presence of one implies that of the other. Indeed, there are also female flowers. With some species, such as hazel, these more closely resemble conventional flowers, being coloured, but they are single, very small, sit close to the tree bark, and they also lack petals. They're unobtrusive and you have to look quite hard to see them. Oaks bear yellow male catkins and the female flowers are reddish in colour and form inconspicuous spikes. On other trees, such as willows, the female flowers are also catkins, but they're green and fairly uninteresting in appearance, except to botanists, I suppose.

The catkins appear before the leaves. That's why we interpret them as harbingers of spring, but that's just us. It's not the tree's reason. The trees, after all, haven't the foggiest idea what we think of them, couldn't care less anyway, and certainly aren't going to perform tricks for our amusement. No, the catkins appear before the leaves so they'll be fully exposed to the wind. Absolutely, they don't want the leaves to shelter them. That would spoil the entire scheme.

Their quivering in the breeze provides a clue. Each male floret along the catkin bears stamens topped with anthers and it produces copious quantities of dry, powdery pollen. The breeze, or better still a somewhat stronger wind, detaches the pollen and sends it whirling through the air. Eventually, since what goes up must come down, the pollen falls to the ground or, with slightly better luck, collides with a solid surface and sticks to it. It may be that the surface it strikes is the stigma of a female flower of the same species. Contact has been made. Fertilization can proceed. Seeds will be produced. There will be progeny.

The catkin-quiverers aren't alone, either. Look around you at the coniferous trees, the firs, pines, spruces, hemlocks, junipers, larches, and all their brethren. They're not flowering plants and their reproductive methods are different and more complicated, but they still produce pollen and they rely on the wind to disperse it.

It's all completely impossible, of course. Think about it. Pollen blows away from the catkins hanging prettily on one tree. It may travel in any direction, be carried to any height – and pollen routinely turns up in air samples collected at heights of several kilometres – the direction may change at random, possibly several times, and yet that pollen is completely wasted unless it just happens to land on the sticky stigma of a female flower that could be anywhere. It's a method of fertilization invented by an idiot. Why do these benighted, misled, conned, swindled plants persist in such perverse behaviour? Well, if you take evolution by natural selection seriously, only one answer is possible: it's utterly preposterous, but it works. There really are hazels along the hedgerows and in the woods. You can see them. Oaks, birches, beeches, alders and all the rest not only survive, they prosper. As old trees die new ones replace them. Female hazels and beeches bear nuts beloved of squirrels. Oaks bear acorns. Sweet chestnuts bear chestnuts, and horse chestnuts bear conkers on which small boys have depended since long before the dawn of history.

Wind pollination is clearly successful, but all the same some plants, most notably certain species of willows, hedge their bets. Some willow species are exclusively wind-pollinated and others are exclusively insect-pollinated, but many use both methods. In those that attract insects, both males and females produce nectar and release a scent, and their catkins are upright, rigid, and highly visible. Scientists have found that the dual strategy seems to work best for willows growing in mountainous regions, where there's usually a wind blowing, but there are fewer insects than there are in the lowlands. So why don't exclusively insect-pollinated mountain willows give up on the insects and rely entirely on the wind? No one knows.

But the really big time anemophiles – anemophily is the technical term for wind-pollination – are everywhere around us. We walk on them, except where we're exhorted not to, and we eat their seeds every day. They are, of course, the grasses. Grasses first appeared on Earth approximately 55 million years ago. That sounds a long time, but measured against the 4.6-billion-year age of our planet it's really no time at all. Yet in that short time they've spread all over the world. Today there are more than 11,300 species of them and they're found on every continent (although there aren't so many in Antarctica). And we'd be in a poor way without them. They supply, quite literally, the bread of life, not to mention the pasta, corn fritters and rice. And the beer and whisky that wash it down. They also feed our cattle and sheep, which are grazers, and farmed chickens are fed maize seed. So the cream in your coffee is a special case of grass. All flesh is grass, as the prophet Isaiah first observed (Isaiah 40:6) and many have repeated without acknowledging the source. Sugar cane is a grass and so is the bamboo on which giant pandas dine and whose stems are arguably the world's most useful natural product, employed for construction, furniture, baskets, and to prop up wobbly garden plants.

Grass flowers are fairly familiar, of course. They're feathery, green ripening to beige, and they wave gracefully in the wind. They come in a wide range of sizes and a variety of shapes, from early sandgrass (*Mibora minima*), which grows up to fifteen centimetres (six inches) including the flower, to the huge, fan-like panicles of pampas grasses, standing up to three metres (ten feet) tall. When Spanish explorers moved inland from the South American coast and encountered the pampa for the first time it's said they had to stand on the backs of their horses to see over the top of the grasses. And what did they see? They saw a sea of grass. It was everywhere.

There are three basic designs of grass flower – racemes, panicles and spikes – and all are inflorescences formed from many florets. Wheat, rye and barley flowers form spikes, with the florets packed tightly along a vertical stem. Rice flowers form panicles in which the florets are separated, each on its own stalk, with the floret stalks branching from bigger stems growing from the main axis of the inflorescence. If the

Grasses have flowers that lack petals. This is bread wheat
(*Triticum aestivum*, also known as *T. vulgare*), an annual grass.

floret stalks arise directly from the main axis the inflorescence is a raceme. In all three designs the florets form spikelets, a spikelet comprising one or more florets attached to an axis called a rachilla.

Grasses are wind-pollinated and have no need to attract pollinating animals so their flowers are reduced to the barest biological minimum as shown by this spikelet comprising florets branching from a main axis.

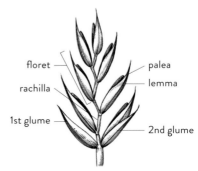

floret

palea

rachilla

lemma

1st glume

2nd glume

At the base of the florets there are one or two bracts called glumes that enclose and protect the florets until they're mature, and another set of two bracts, the lemma outside the floret and the palea on the inside, protect each floret. In some grasses bristle-like extensions called awns project from the tips of the lemma and palea. There are no sepals or petals. Instead, there are two more scales called lodicules. These expand and contract to spread wide the lemma and palea, opening the floret.

In most grasses the florets contain both male and female organs. There's an ovary with two feathery stigmas rising from it, and below the ovary three stamens. Maize (corn) is the most notable exception to this arrangement. It bears separate male and female flowers.

When the flowers mature, in early summer, the warm breeze wafts away the microscopically tiny pollen grains from the grass flowers. Away they fly, in invisible clouds that drift this way and that, over the fields and woods, and into the towns, and the gardens, and the parks, and the homes, and the offices, and the schools, into eyes, up noses, and into bronchii.

Pollen fills the air, more or less of it according to the atmospheric conditions, and although no one can see it we soon know all about it. Weather forecasts include predictions of pollen counts and send the victims of hay fever heading for cover and checking their supplies of medication as the season of misery, red eyes and snuffles threatens to envelop them. It wouldn't be anything like so bad if the grasses could manage to release less of the stuff, but to be fair, they aren't the only offenders. All those anemophilic trees play a part, too. Whole plantations of conifers are hard at it, square kilometre after square kilometre of them. The grasses get most of the blame because there's so many of them and they all flower at about the same time. And, of course, most sufferers are more sensitive to some types of pollen than to others.

Alas, there's not a thing we can do about it. It's the way it works. An anemophile doesn't have to bother with or, more to the point, go to the expense of attracting pollinating animals. It doesn't need to invest resources in sugar-rich nectar. It has no use for sepals or petals. Its flowers are reduced to the barest biological minimum. If colourful flower arrangements provide the subject matter for countless still lifes, wind-pollinated flowers attract the minimalists, the lovers of understated simple elegance. These are the most refined of flowers. Aesthetes should bow before them.

Lacking little winged helpers to transport their pollen to where it's meant to go, grasses must rely on the unpredictable wind. Their pollen goes all over the place and it's a matter of purest chance whether it reaches a compatible stigma. The odds are shortened, naturally, where grasses are the predominant plants over vast areas. Pollen from a prairie grass may well reach a friendly female on grasslands that extend from Manitoba to Alberta. But farmers plough up the grasslands to grow wheat and over in Europe grasses flower only along roadside verges, in nature reserves, and on localized areas of wasteland. Fortunately for the grasses, the solution to this is simple. They produce truly humungous quantities of pollen. This presents no problems to them, because pollen is cheap. A pollen grain is tiny, it's not made of much, so plants can produce as much of it as they need. Those that get the production level right will find and fertilize females, produce seeds, and prosper. Those that produce too little will father fewer seeds, so their populations will decrease. That's natural selection for you.

But the pollination season doesn't last forever. At last the pollenated sky clears, the hay fever victims breathe easier, and the plants get on with the business of making seeds and fruit.

Grasses scatter their seeds all around them and some of those seeds are able to bury themselves while they wait to germinate, below ground where the birds and mice won't find them. They do this by flexing their awns in response to changes in the humidity of the air, and their bending and straightening awns drag them down.

It all works out very well, but when our ancestors first started to cultivate annual grasses with edible seeds they encountered a difficulty. As soon as the seeds were ripe, the plant scattered them, making them very difficult to collect. Going out with your flint-edged sickle to cut the stalks would simply scatter the seeds more. But some plants were better than others at the seed-scattering business, which meant the harvesters could gather those that still held on to their seeds, take them to a central place, and thresh them to gather the seeds – the grain. They kept a proportion of that grain to sow, and with repeated sowing over generations there developed plants that had lost the knack of scattering their grain. And so those early farmers developed our cultivated cereals, and the cereals we grow today are utterly dependent on us for their survival and differ substantially from their wild ancestors. They can't scatter their seeds, which means they're unable to survive in the wild. In fact, we've genetically modified them, as we have most of our food plants, of course.

Male, female, or both
—

Gender is a nuanced concept. It's not simply a matter of determining whether an individual is male or female. There are degrees, a gradient. But we get by, most of the time, most of us.

When it comes to reproduction rather than relationships, however, it's fairly straightforward for animals. You need a male and a female and a bit of luck. True, there are animals, such as aphids, that go in for parthenogenesis – virgin birth – and some that change gender in the course of their lives, but these are the exceptions and there aren't that many of them. So it's only natural to assume the same goes for plants – to produce seeds you need male flowers and female flowers and a conjugation of the two. If a flower has anthers it's male, if it's got ovaries it's female, so how can there be a problem?

Well, it's not quite that simple because, you will recall from the description of flowers and the explanation of how they work, there are flowers that possess both male and female organs. Plants bearing such flowers are hermaphrodites, both male and female, so they can perform as either, and that option generates a rather longer list of possible genders. There are hermaphrodites, which are male and female in the same flower. Then there are monoecious plants, which produce separate male and female flowers but all on the same plant. There are dioecious plants, which bear male and female flowers on separate plants, andromonoecious plants that bear both hermaphrodite and male flowers on the same plant, gynomonoecious plants that bear both hermaphrodite and female flowers on the same plant, and a few mixtures. There are species of hermaphrodite plants that also have separate male and female individuals, not to mention monoecious species that also produce separate male and female plants. This adds up to at least seven possible combinations, or genders.

Speaking from the point of view of an animal restricted to a mere two genders, you might think the plants are being a bit self-indulgent here, but at least you'd expect them to content themselves with their seven or more genders. And most do, but not all of them, and a few are seriously weird. Consider the curious case of the papaya or pawpaw, the pear-shaped fruit with the orange flesh and black seeds that can't make up its mind what it's called, which is suspicious for a start. As the picture shows, papaya fruits grow in bunches on an attractive, pretty regular-looking tree. It's a native of tropical America, but it's grown in warm climates in many other parts of the world, commercially and in private gardens. And, of course, you can buy papaya fruits in any supermarket.

Papaya trees decided long ago that they weren't going to restrict themselves to such a limited choice of boringly predictable sexual arrangements. There are, then, papaya trees with male flowers, papaya trees with female flowers, and papaya trees with hermaphrodite flowers, and some trees stick with these and spend their entire lives as males, females, or hermaphrodites. Then there are some that choose to complicate things. A papaya tree may have a mixture of male and hermaphrodite, or female and hermaphrodite, or all three male, female, and hermaphrodite flowers.

That gives you a fair number of possible combinations, but not enough to satisfy the exotic predilections of the papaya. You could say it has great trouble making up its mind. Or it would if it had a mind. Maybe gender counselling might help?

Most plants settle down with the gender they inherit and make do with that, but not the papaya. Male papaya trees may start producing hermaphrodite flowers. Gardeners who buy and plant a papaya tree only to find it's male and produces no fruit can remedy the situation by giving the tree a good, hard bash or two, preferably, they say, with a cutlass. If you can't remember where you left your cutlass, perhaps a few whacks

Papaya or pawpaw (*Carica papaya*), native to tropical America but cultivated extensively elsewhere, occurs in 31 distinct genders.

with a spade might do the trick. Then there are hermaphrodite papaya trees that suddenly decide to produce female flowers as well, and trees with hermaphrodite and male flowers that start producing female flowers instead of the male ones.

It's all to do with the chromosomes, you see. Like vertebrate animals, plants have X and Y sex chromosomes and inherit one chromosome from each parent. An individual inheriting XX is female, and one inheriting XY is male. However, the papaya asserts its originality by possessing a third type of chromosome, designated Y2. Add Y2 chromosomes to the X and Y mix and gender-bending is the inevitable result. Thus, if a male tree mates with a hermaphrodite the resulting seeds produce equal numbers of hermaphrodites, males, and females, and if a female tree mates with a hermaphrodite there are no males among the progeny, only females and hermaphrodites. Got all that? When you work out all the possible permutations you find that papayas have 31 genders to choose from. And that's more than enough for anyone.

"When you work out all the possible permutations, papayas have 31 genders to choose from."

As you'll have gathered by now, hermaphrodite and monoecious plants are able to fertilize themselves. That can be an advantage, because the pollinators may pass by unimpressed by the goodies on offer, and the wind, ever unreliable, may scatter the pollen widely, but in the wrong direction and many kilometres from a genetically compatible female plant. So self-fertilization, or selfing, is a useful fall-back strategy, and one that pays off. A team of ecologists led by Dena Grossenbacher at the University of Minnesota Twin Cities studied data on the geographic distribution of plants from hundreds of species in twenty genera and fifteen families and found a consistent pattern. Selfers – species that reproduce by self-fertilization – occur over larger ranges than species that require a mating partner. Selfers also establish themselves in higher latitudes than related non-selfers, and the difference in the size of their ranges has increased over time since the selfers and closely related non-selfers diverged evolutionarily.

So selfing works, but as we saw in the section on the purpose of sex, there's a serious downside. Repeated inbreeding is detrimental. Researchers have found with crop plants that after about four generations of selfing the plants are smaller and produce less seed, and outbreeding immediately restores both their size and productivity. Consequently, most plants use selfing sparingly and have ways of avoiding it.

The hermaphrodite primrose has found an ingenious solution. Next time the primroses bloom, examine the flowers closely and you'll find that although they appear identical from a distance, in fact there are two different types. Look directly down into the flower and you'll see that the petals are joined together at the base, where they form a tube. At their centre you may see a green, roughly circular, disc-like structure with a yellowy-orange tangle below it. The green disc is the stigma, the structure below it is the anthers, and the stigma is clearly at the top. Because the stigma looks a little like a pinhead and is about the same size, this flower is known as the pin type. Alternatively, at the centre of the petals you may see the yellowy-orange anthers. This is the thrum type of flower and the stigma is below it.

So how does this work? Insects visit primroses in search of nectar, which is located at the bottom of the tube at the base of the flower, so when one alights it has to reach all the way down with its long 'tongue', its proboscis. If it's alighted on a pin-eyed flower any pollen already sticking to its proboscis from its last feed will wipe off on to the stigma at the top, and the insect will acquire more pollen on its proboscis from the anthers halfway down. If the insect alights on a thrum-eyed flower the pollen on the end of its proboscis is in the right position to meet the stigma halfway down and more pollen will cling to the middle of the proboscis. Charles Darwin was the first scientist to observe this difference in primrose flowers, and he also noted that pollen grains from pin flowers are smaller than those from thrum flowers. Just to make sure, however, thrums produce large pollen and pins small pollen, making it difficult for pollen of one type to engage successfully with the stigma of a flower of the same type, thus reducing the likelihood of self-pollination. In addition, genetic differences between the two types ensure that sperm cannot fertilize flowers of the same type.

If the pin and thrum distinction works, then in a clump of primroses there should be similar numbers of pin and thrum flowers. And there are. You can check for yourself.

Avocados *(Persea americana)*, we're told, are as close as you'll get to the perfect food. Positively bursting with fibre, vitamins, and other goodies, they contain pretty much everything you need for good health and a long life. They grow on broad-leaved evergreen trees related to laurels that originated in Central America and are widely cultivated in warm parts of the world. Avocado trees bear hermaphrodite flowers and have devised a truly ingenious way to avoid selfing.

There are two types of avocado tree – let's call them A and B. On type A trees the flowers open in the morning as females, with their stigmas receptive and anthers out of the way. The flowers close at midday and remain closed until the afternoon of the following day, when they reopen as males, their anthers now loaded with pollen and their stigmas unreceptive. Type B trees match them by opening their flowers in the afternoon as females, closing them at night, and reopening them the following morning as males. It means neither type of tree can pollinate itself because its male and female reproductive organs are never functional at the same time. The trees have to outbreed, A with B and B with A. What's more, by alternating gender both A- and B-type trees

Some flowers of the avocado (*Persea americana*) open in the afternoon as females, close at night, and reopen the following morning as males. Others open in the morning as females, close at midday, and reopen as males the following afternoon.

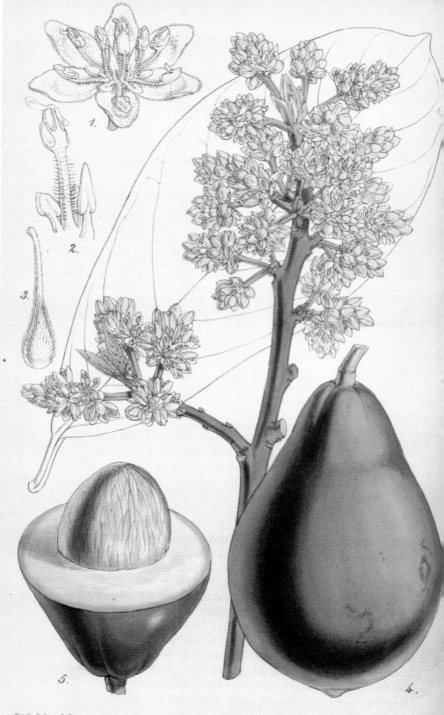

2.

3.

5.

4.

Fitch, del et lith.

Reeve & Nichols imp

bear fruit and therefore produce seeds, which puts them a couple of steps ahead of the rest of us. Neat, don't you think?

Sometimes a plant can lose control of its own gender. This happens when an invading organism alters the machinery for its own ends. It's inadvertent, of course; the invader has no interest in the doings of its host. It happens to campion, the summer flower of meadow and hedgerow.

There are two hybridizing campions, red (*Silene dioica*) and white (*S. latifolia*), as well as other *Silene* species found in eastern North America, and the invader is *Microbotryum lychnis-dioicae* (formerly called *Ustilago violacea*), a parasitic fungus found all over Europe and North America. The fungus infects flower anthers, feeding on them and taking them over completely. Infected flowers often last longer than those that remain uninfected and even after the petals of infected flowers have withered the filaments are still strong. Eventually, though, the diseased anthers explode, releasing showers of fungal spores.

That's one way the fungus spreads its progeny, but it does better, at least from its own point of view. Campions are dioecious, bearing male and female flowers on separate plants. When the fungus alights on a female plant it triggers the development of stamen-like structures called staminodes. In other words, the female flower becomes a male. Apparently the fungus achieves this magical transmutation by behaving chemically like a Y chromosome. The female flowers lack a Y chromosome and supplying one renders them male, although they're male flowers that still retain their female parts, albeit these are repressed. And, of course, the newly male flowers don't make good campion fathers, not at all. The fungus has only one purpose in conjuring staminodes – that's to produce more fungus, to which end it fills the 'anthers' with its spores. They still look like anthers, though, at least if you're an insect. Flies and bees visit in search of a meal and leave unsatisfied, but their visit sprinkles them with fungal spores, which they carry with them to the next uninfected campion flower, thereby spreading the fungus. It's a free service they provide, and once it starts it won't be long before all the neighbouring campions are infected, quite ruining the neighbourhood.

Goings-on among the wildflowers are interesting and throw up some curiosities, but they're not really important, in the sense that they don't affect the bottom line. No one grows campions for sale, after all, but when commerce becomes involved steps have to be taken. You can't just leave these plants to get on with it and hope for the best. That won't pay for the riding lessons and the accountant's Merc.

Hand pollination is simple enough, if tedious, for fruit crops. It involves collecting pollen from the anthers of the male flowers, usually using a fine paintbrush, and transferring it to the stigmas of the female flowers. If the plants are monoecious – separate male and female flowers on the same plant – shaking the plant gently may be enough to dislodge pollen that will float on to the nearby stigmas. These techniques will help increase the number of fruits by ensuring all the female flowers are fertilized, and often the size of the fruit as well. Growers use hand pollination to improve yields of such crops as cucumbers, squashes, peppers, and aubergines. Obviously it's not needed for leaf or root crops, such as carrots, parsnips, turnips, or brassicas, because unless you're growing them to produce seeds for sale, you'll harvest them before they flower. Pollination never happens. Artificial hand pollination is applied mainly to crops grown in greenhouses or hydroponically.

Tree fruits also need pollinators and often benefit from a little assistance. If you're a billionaire running a big corporation you can do the job in style by buying in sacks of pollen and scattering the grains from an aircraft. Or you can hire beekeepers to bring their hives on to your property and let the bees do the job. One day there'll be a hi-tech method using battery-powered, insect-sized robot bees, beebots, that will buzz merrily about the orchards, tirelessly shifting pollen from tree to tree, eating none of it, seeking no nectar, and asking only to be plugged into a wall socket when they feel a bit depleted. And they won't sting, ever. Teams of engineers are working on it at this very moment.

CHAPTER 4

BOOZERS
AND
CHANCERS

Meet the unsavoury characters, including
drunks, substance abusers and chancers that
go hand-in-hand with plant reproduction.

Drunks and other substance abusers

—

As everyone knows, it's a basic law of nature that if something can go wrong it will, and if it can't it will anyway. Flowering plants produce nectar to reward pollinators, and nectar is mainly sugar. And that's a problem, because if certain yeasts find their way into a sugar solution they'll feed contentedly on the sugar, producing alcohol as a by-product, and they'll go on doing so until they've converted so much of the sugar into alcohol that their own metabolic waste poisons them. That's fermentation, and it's how we make all our alcoholic beverages. The process also happens all by itself, especially in warm climates, because fermentation proceeds best if the sugar solution is kept warm. So when animals visit certain flowers in search of nectar, the plants supply booze to their potential pollinators. It's not illegal, despite the plants having no licence, because they're not selling the liquor or taking it across national frontiers, so no customs duty is chargeable on it. All the same, we must ask, is it ethical? Obviously, the befuddled visitors don't complain so it's up to us to watch out for their best interests.

At flowering time the Bertram palm (*Eugeissona tristis*), a tree found in the rainforests of Thailand, Malaysia and Borneo, turns itself into a bar. Some of the trees lack stems and grow in dense clusters and these stemless trees produce huge, erect, woody inflorescences, up to three metres (ten feet) tall, comprising equal numbers of hermaphrodite and male florets. Both types of floret appear at the same time and both produce copious amounts of nectar for five or six weeks while the florets are maturing. Then nectar production ceases and the flowers expose pollen for one day only before closing down production of both nectar and pollen for about six weeks. After that, nectar production resumes and the cycle repeats, until at last the stigmas mature and fruit can form.

While they're producing nectar the inflorescences smell like a brewery and the liquid froths, showing that the nectar is fermenting vigorously, thanks to a resident community of yeast species. When fermentation ends the nectar has an alcohol content of up to 3.8 per cent, which is about that of a weak beer.

Once the brew is ready it's opening time and one by one the regulars start to arrive, gathering pollen in their fur as they climb around imbibing. The pen-tailed tree shrews are heavy drinkers. Each of them spends more than two hours every night drinking steadily, but they're inured to an intake that would make a person drunk if they consumed an equivalent amount scaled up for the difference in body size. When it's time to leave, the tree shrew doesn't reel or stagger, far less fall down or start fighting. It's not particular about the bar it frequents, and may well patronize a different flower the next night, possibly delivering some of the pollen still caught in its fur. These small mammals acquired their name from the bushy fur at the ends of their tails, which looks like a quill pen.

"The pen-tailed tree shrews are heavy drinkers, imbibing enough alcohol for their body weight to make a human drunk."

Tree shrews are not related to the shrews you might find in your garden. They're primates, and you and I are descended from a primate rather like a tree shrew. What's more, many other primates, including monkeys, will drink alcohol when the opportunity arises. Vervet monkeys, for instance, drink fermented sugar cane, and they do get drunk. Since we're primates, too, does this suggest that we're descended from a long line of boozers? And does it suggest that boozing is an entirely natural thing to do, that pubs and bars are integral to our natural habitat? It's a thought.

Slow lorises, which are also primates, turn up at Bertram's Bar for a drink or two at different times of day and night.

J.Smit del et lith .

2 .

Mintern Bros . imp.

FACES OF LORISES.

LEFT: The pen-tailed tree shrew (*Ptilocercus lowii*), a native of the forests of south-east Asia, boozes all day. Its name refers to the quill-like tuft of hair at the tip of its tail.
ABOVE: The slow loris (*Nycticebus coucang*) at the bottom of this plate is another heavy drinker of fermented nectar, but the liquor doesn't seem to make it drunk.

They drink more at night than they do during the day, often taking as many as nine drinks in the course of an evening. Like the tree shrews, the slow lorises don't seem at all incapacitated when leaving.

Business is quieter by day. Common tree shrews often call by, as well as plantain squirrels. Night-time customers also include several species of rats.

Birds try to stay off the stuff. They don't handle it well and whereas mammals can walk home from the bar, birds have to fly, and they're simply not up to it when they've had a few. Liquor and aviation don't mix. Sometimes, though, they're tempted, or maybe they're just thirsty and can't find water. Whatever the reason, it happens. In the tropical north of Australia, as the dry season approaches its end and a number of trees open flowers offering abundant nectar, the birds fall victim. Nectar ferments in the heat and red-collared lorikeets (*Trichoglossus rubritorquis*) are especially drawn to it. People find them lying around, dishevelled, quite incapable of flying and barely able to walk. Kind folk pick them up, drunk and incapable, and take them to veterinarians, where they sleep it off.

Various trees contribute to the inebriation of the local fauna, but the main offender is probably *Schotia brachypetala*, a tree that grows naturally only in parts of southern Africa but has been planted elsewhere as an ornamental and is especially popular among gardeners in Darwin. You can buy its seeds online and it's not difficult to grow, provided you live in the tropics, of course. It has various common names, including weeping boer-bean, African walnut and tree fuchsia, but it's probably best known as the drunken parrot tree, and we know why. Weeping boer-bean is also appropriate. The tree is a member of the bean family, right enough, it grows in South Africa, and it weeps. If you shake it when its deep red flowers are open it will drip thick, sticky, sweet nectar that otherwise oozes from the flowers. It's not surprising, then, that the tree attracts all kinds of birds and insects.

If you're a plant you have to face the fact that you live in a world of herbivores, mobile beings that regard you as lunch.

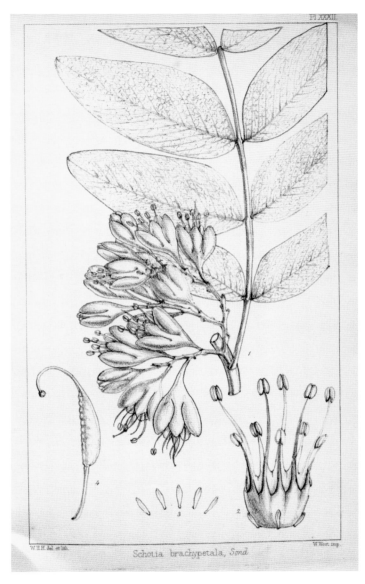

PL XXXII

W.H.H. del. et lith.

Schotia brachypetala, Sond

W.West imp.

The drunken parrot tree (*Schotia brachypetala*)
has several other names, but owes this one
to the unfortunate effect its fermented nectar
has on parrots that drink it.

This is clearly a problem, but there are things you can do about it to make sure you keep healthy and live long enough to produce flowers and seeds. One is to produce poisons. It's best if the poison doesn't kill the animal that takes a bite out of you, because then it would learn nothing. On the other hand, if the poison simply makes the aggressor feel dreadful it will learn to leave you and other plants that look like you strictly alone. What's more, with a bit of luck it will teach its offspring to give you a wide berth as well, with the happy result that your only animal visitors will be the pollinators you invite.

Only, yet again, there's a risk you'll run up against the law of unintended consequences. Some beastly beasts may develop a taste for the very weapon you're trying to hit them with.

Take opium. Or rather, don't on any account take opium. It is the poison with which opium poppies aim to deter grazers. As you may know, the scent from a field of poppies sent Dorothy to sleep on her way to call on the Wizard of Oz, and she's not the only victim. However, pharmaceutical companies need a supply of opium for their research, so someone has to grow opium poppies legally. Australian farmers are responsible for a significant proportion of these research poppies, great fields of them just like the field that zapped Dorothy. Dorothy wasn't Australian, of course, but wallabies are and they can get seriously hooked. They walk into the fields, eat the flowers, then wander around aimlessly until they collapse, and their crashing around causes considerable damage to the crop, so the authorities try to stop them. It's the crop they're bothered about, mind, not the wallabies, which are hopeless addicts.

Early in the year, when there's not much grass or many herbs, grazing animals may be tempted to eat one of about twenty species of legumes known collectively as locoweeds. What these plants share in common is a toxin called swainsonine. When horses, cattle or sheep ingest swainsonine it has a calming effect on them at first. They tend to stand as though transfixed, seemingly sunk deep in thought the way Socrates used to stand for hours on end, except, of course, that in this case their minds almost certainly are completely blank, because they don't do deep thought. This is harmless enough, but if the grazers persist in their locoweed consumption, after a couple of weeks they'll start to lose weight, miscarry, and their behaviour may become unpredictable and sometimes violent. Then they're definitely loco. Eventually this locoism can be fatal.

In contrast, catnip will send most cats into paroxysms of delight but without doing them any harm, because they know when they've had enough. Not all cats succumb to it, and young kittens don't like it, but apart from domestic moggies it appeals strongly to all of their big relatives, even lions and tigers. It makes them purr, roll on the ground, chew the flowers and leaves, and generally behave in a loopy fashion. If they eat a lot of it they're likely to drool idiotically and leap around. It's possible that the plant makes them hallucinate, because they may start hunting mice that only they can see. Before long, though, the attraction wears off and they become bored as only a cat can.

Catnip's active ingredient is called nepelalactone and it's secreted by the leaves and stems of several plants in the genus *Nepeta*, but especially *N. cataria*, a perennial herb that's easy to grow and that bears pretty, perfumed flowers. Butterflies also like the plant, but it's the flowers that attract them and they're pollinators. If you're really keen to try it too you can brew a herbal tea from it.

The chancers

—

When disaster leaves the land bare, its covering of plants swept, burned, or blasted away, the resulting scene of utter devastation depresses the spirit. After fire or an air raid has done its work of destroying homes, lives, and livelihoods, there is little the shocked, disoriented former occupants can do but pick haphazardly through the rubble hoping against hope to find something, anything, a memento, a souvenir, that might link them to the world they have lost forever.

If the disaster falls in spring or summer, though, it's not long, often no more than a week or two, before the first plant appears. It grows tall and opens racemes of bright mauve to pink flowers that bring the promise of life returning. And that plant is not isolated. Its fellows spring up everywhere until they occupy every last corner that receives at least a modicum of sunlight, for they cannot tolerate deep shade, and soon the areas they occupy are buzzing and fluttering with the insects eager to sup on their nectar. When they've drunk their fill and the pollen has been distributed, clouds of tiny seeds carried on fine hairs float away through the streets and over the rooftops. The very sight of these plants and their insect companions confirms the resilience of the natural world. Life is not so easily extinguished.

Where that plant leads others will surely follow and unless people bring them under control by starting to cultivate the ground, within a year or less the bare ground will have become an impenetrable jungle of nettles, brambles, and a hundred other wild plants. But by then that first beacon of hope will have long gone, its progeny seeking other land recently cleared of buildings and, more relevant to the plant, cleared of rival plants.

Some people call the plant fireweed and during World War Two its rapid colonization of bombsites earned it the name bombweed. It grows throughout temperate and subarctic regions, and on mountains in the tropics and subtropics.

Londoners have chosen it to symbolize their city and since 1957 it has been the official floral emblem of Yukon, Canada. It is best known in Britain as rosebay willowherb and in Canada as great willowherb, and it's one of the most familiar of all wild plants.

Ecologists describe rosebay willowherb as a pioneer plant. By that they mean it's a chancer, a plant that appears rapidly on ground that has been cleared of other vegetation, spreads rapidly, matures, and produces copious quantities of seed that it distributes before rival plants have had time to grow up and shade it. Then it disappears. At least, it disappears from sight. Some of its seeds, those that have not flown far away across the squares, mansions, and terraces, the rail tracks or forest, remain viable in the soil for many years, waiting for the next occasion when its rivals will be defeated and the willowherb can flourish.

Even if you don't know its name, you'll know what it looks like. You'll have seen it on any summer rail journey, because it loves railroad embankments, and you'll also be familiar with it growing on roadside verges. It arrives on these sites while they're still fresh and the ground is disturbed, and it survives there because of human intervention to cut down tall, woody plants that might prove dangerous to travellers and, incidentally, would shade out the light-loving willowherb. Walk through the forest and you'll see it there, too, growing in clearings and beside many of the footpaths.

We may love it in times of hardship and danger, or in prosperous times see it as a sign of neglect, growing in city spaces that we feel ought to be put to better use, but the willowherb, of course, has no concern for us or our sentiments. It's not courting our popularity and it's indifferent to our scorn. Its only concern is the same as that of all its rivals, the other plants. It needs to produce seeds, and fast.

Once its seeds have germinated the plant grows rapidly to a height of up to two metres (six and a half feet), or occasionally higher under really ideal conditions. There is a very similar species, dwarf willowherb, that grows to only about sixty

Rosebay willowherb (*Chamerion* [formerly *Epilobium*] *angustifolium*) is quick to appear on disturbed sites with little or no other vegetation.

centimetres (two feet). As either willowherb grows, the plant extends its root system and also rhizomes – underground stems – with nodes from which more plants arise, so that what begins as a single plant can come to form a large stand of plants, all linked below ground. This is how a few initial plants are able to spread to occupy the whole site.

When it flowers, rosebay willowherb opens its florets a few at a time, starting at the bottom and moving up. Each floret begins as a male. After a time, the pollen gone from its anthers, the stamens wither and then the stigma opens. There are always male and female flowers sexually active at the same time, but never on the same plant. The flowers attract a wide variety of insects, especially honeybees, bumblebees and butterflies.

Then the willowherb produces its fruits. These are tubular capsules up to eight centimetres (three inches) long, covered in hairs, and each capsule contains up to four hundred seeds. That means each plant produces up to 80,000 seeds and, remember, the plant you see is but one of a stand of plants growing from the rhizomes, so that genetically they're identical, a single plant. A plume of silky hairs surrounds each seed and when the capsules burst open the air fills with white clouds of seeds floating on the breeze, drifting away, most of them remaining airborne until the rain washes them to the ground, where they lodge and remain, dormant, until some catastrophe clears away the surrounding plants and they can seize their chance.

A single tubular fruit of the willowherb contains up to 400 seeds which means each plant produces up to 80,000 seeds.

Farm livestock can eat rosebay willowherb and, indeed, some farmers say it increases milk yield and add it to cattle feed. People can eat the young stalks, raw or cooked like asparagus, and you can add the young leaves to salads. But be careful you don't mistake it for any of the many poisonous wild plants that may be growing nearby. Be sure you know your plants!

Naturally, you wouldn't expect the willowherb to have everything its own way. Its pioneering strategy – germinate fast, grow and spread fast, produce vast quantities of small, light seeds, and disperse them on the wind – is very successful, but it's also fairly obvious. If you're a plant, of course. Others have opted for it, and it's never long before some of them appear among the stands of willowherb, but it's usually the willowherb that establishes itself first.

Which plants arrive depends on the type of site, but on disturbed ground many will belong to the aster family. You might see beggar-ticks (*Bidens pilosa*), known in different parts of Britain as black-jack, Spanish needle and cobbler's pegs, a plant with pale yellow flowers that grows as tall as a man. Foxgloves will turn up, and stinging nettles, and after a while the first of the woody plants. Very often this is buddleia, the butterfly bush, springing up from its tiny, wind-borne seeds. You may also see relatives of rosebay willowherb, such as great hairy willowherb, which some people call codlins-and-cream. This is very similar in size and appearance, but usually confined to wet ground in places such as riverbanks.

Rosebay willowherb is a gentle plant, with a gentle name, and its stands shelter new arrivals that grow more slowly. As these cast their shade, the willowherb disappears gracefully, its task complete. But not all pioneers are so well-mannered, and at least two are aggressive bullies. Spotted knapweed, originally a native of eastern Europe, was introduced to North America around the end of the nineteenth century and it has become a seriously invasive weed, covering millions of acres, as has its cousin diffuse knapweed, originally from eastern

Europe and the Middle East, which reached North America early in the twentieth century.

As befits a pioneer, knapweed produces hundreds or thousands of tiny seeds that drift on the wind borne on hairs, much like willowherb seeds, but that's not how it spreads. Deer and other mammals eat the seed heads of young plants – older plants are tough and unpalatable – but don't digest the seeds, which they distribute in their faeces. Don't blame the grazers entirely, though, because people are the main distributors. Drive through a patch of knapweed in your off-road vehicle and up to 2000 seeds may lodge on the underside, then fall off, a few at a time, as you speed away. Seeds are also distributed during road construction, when topsoil is removed and deposited elsewhere.

The seeds germinate on disturbed ground and the knapweed's root system forms a relationship with a soil fungus. Between them, the roots and fungus absorb nutrients from the vicinity of nearby grass roots, killing the grass and allowing the knapweed to spread. As is the case with many invasive species, grasses in its original homeland evolved alongside it and were able to cope. American grasses, never having encountered it, were helpless, and once knapweed arrives it's very difficult to remove it.

CHAPTER 5

BRIBES

———

Pollen, perfume and pongs – three devices plants
use to lure insects to their flowers.

Bees and butterflies

—

As you lie dozing among the too-long grass on a warm summer afternoon, blind to the judgmental mower glowering silently in the corner, just take a moment or two, for you have plenty, to listen to the buzzing of the insects. Look at those insects individually, though, and you'll find that most of them manage to fly perfectly well without buzzing. It's the bees and wasps that do most of the buzzing, and the volume of their buzzing, now your ear's attuned, is a clear indication of the sheer number of them. They're all around you, working away among the flowers, and they buzz because they move their wings so rapidly when they fly – about 230 wing beats per second. Other insects flap less frenetically. John Milton likened the buzz to the bee's song:

> 'While the bee with honied thigh,
> That at her flowery work doth sing,
> And the waters murmuring
> With such consort as they keep,
> Entice the dewy-feather'd sleep.'
> (*Il Penderoso*, I, 142)

It's not a song and bees don't carry honey on their thighs, so maybe Milton was a better poet than he was a naturalist, but you know what he meant and it's because we like honey and the sugar rush it can deliver that bees have played such an important part in our culture since those distant times when there were no other sources of almost pure sugar. Most ancient civilizations had bee gods and even bee-atheists should treat bees with respect. If you keep bees you should always tell them of important family events, such as births, marriages, and deaths. They'll be offended if you don't, and they might high tail it off to somewhere else. Domesticated they may be, but a hive of honeybees has a collective mind of its own. They call it swarm intelligence.

There are at least 25,000 species of bees in the world as a whole, with about 4000 in North America and 254 in Britain, of which 24 are bumblebees. Not all of them live in colonies populous enough to produce quantities of honey people would think worth stealing, but all of them pollinate flowers. There are several species of honeybee, of which the most widespread, and the only one domesticated in Britain and North America, is *Apis mellifera*. There are many more species of wasps, but they're mostly predators or parasites and few of them are much use as pollinators. And that's rather odd, because the ancestors of bees were predatory wasps that devoured other insects. It may be that by feeding on pollinating insects dusted with pollen the bee-ancestors acquired a taste for the stuff and set about collecting it for themselves. Who knows?

No matter how it all began, once the bees turned their attention to flowers, flowers and bees began to evolve together. Early flowers were open, making their nectar and pollen available to insects of all kinds, especially beetles, but once the bees muscled in strange things began to happen. Many flowers became more tube-shaped, their nectar stashed away at the bottom of a deep funnel. In response, the bees developed longer and longer 'tongues' to reach it. This co-evolutionary process made both flowers and bees increasingly specialized. In time the flowers came to depend on bees and the bees on the flowers. It was, you might say, the slow development of one of life's most beautiful friendships.

You might not be able to tell one bee species from another, but it's not difficult to tell the difference between a slim, dark, wasp-like honeybee and a fat, hairy bumblebee. Their yellow-orange and black colouring warns any animal – or person for that matter – that they're dangerous if threatened, armed with a venomous sting. Look closely at a bee as it moves from flower to flower and you may see the lumps of yellow pollen on its hind legs, held by incurved hairs that form pollen baskets. Bees also collect nectar, but they store that internally, in a honey sac.

A honeybee has a fairly short proboscis – its 'tongue' – so it visits the more open flowers with nectar it can reach. It's the bumblebees, with their much longer proboscis, that rummage around in the tubular flowers.

As she buzzes across the roads and fields, the foraging worker honeybee is either searching for food or heading to a patch of flowers one or more of her sisters has identified. A worker who comes across a source of food she considers valuable returns at once to the hive, where she performs a series of movements – the 'bee dance' – to communicate the direction, distance, type, and quality of the food to the community. If another worker has also been there and found that the flowers have now gone or been cleaned out, so flying there is a waste of time and effort, she'll interrupt the dance and stop it, and that will be that. But if the dancer isn't interrupted, and she succeeds in persuading enough of the other workers, a quorum, the bees make a collective decision and a squadron will leave the hive. The bee's big eyes allow her to judge distances and orient herself with regard to the position of the sun as she follows the heading she's been given for the prescribed distance.

The worker bees are all sisters and indeed all the honeybees in a hive are close relatives, but the familial arrangements are not like ours and you may find them, well, peculiar. In the first place, despite all those females, there is only one mother, the queen. A week or two after a new queen is born, she leaves the hive for her mating flight. She's away for several days, during which time she mates with a number of male bees, called drones. Then she returns to the hive and starts laying. And does she lay! With worker bees attending to her every need, the queen lays up to 1500 eggs a day and continues at that rate for the next two to four years, which is as long as she lives. The eggs are fertilized with the sperm she acquired during her mating flight. Towards the end of her life the queen lays eggs that hatch into drones and the workers alter the way they treat a few of the eggs they're tending in order to produce a replacement queen.

Here's where it gets tricky. Drones hatch from unfertilized eggs, so a drone has a mother but no father, and when their sperm fertilizes the eggs carried by a queen, all of those eggs are female. But although a drone has no father, he does have a grandfather, who was the drone that fertilized his mother. Consequently, although the drone can produce only daughters, those of his daughters that become queens can produce sons. The result of all this is that honeybee sisters are related to each other much more closely than are sisters among mammals. And probably it is the closeness of their relationships that accounts for the social structure of the hive, which depends on all the sisters abandoning any possibility of reproducing.

Apart from chasing the virgin queen and trying to mate with her, drones are fairly useless. Not for nothing did P.G. Wodehouse consign his chinless wonders to The Drones' Club. Drones that succeed in having their way with the queen leave their genitalia and tips of their abdomens temporarily blocking her reproductive tract and, having mated, they die from the injury. Those that fail could go out looking for food, but don't bother, and they're not great fliers anyway. They sort of hang around, studiously avoiding all of the chores necessary to the maintenance of the family home, showing not the slightest interest in the eggs and larvae, and expect the workers to feed them. Well, some might say that's males for you. Drones live for a few weeks. Sometimes the workers kill them. A bit drastic, but you can't really blame them.

Workers, in contrast, and rather obviously given their name, do all the work. For the first few days after a new worker emerges from her cocoon, other workers feed and clean her. It takes that long for her body to harden and her wings to strengthen.

Then she starts her career, hive-cleaning, working the wax to make and maintain the honeycomb, and performing the tasks necessary to convert nectar to honey. She'll help with tending the eggs and larvae and looking after the queen, who never moves, taking food to her and carrying away the eggs and placing them in cells in the honeycomb. She'll spend some time on guard duty near the hive entrance, prepared if need be to die repelling invaders, and she'll have to do a turn as the air conditioning. This involves fanning air through the hive by buzzing her wings.

When she's three weeks old the worker is considered old enough and sensible enough to be allowed to go forth into the world as a forager, on short trips at first as she learns her way round, then on longer excursions. She'll bring in supplies of nectar, pollen and propolis. The last is a resin-like substance the bees obtain from sap, buds, and other parts of plants. It's used to seal superfluous entrances to the hive that invaders might exploit, and generally to strengthen the hive structure. If a small animal, such as a mouse or lizard, manages to get into the hive the workers will kill it, but it's too big for them to carry it outside to dispose of it, so they encase it in propolis. Propolis, you can see, has many uses.

The worker's is a busy life, and after about six weeks she dies. In summer an average beehive contains up to 60,000 workers, a few hundred drones, and one queen.

As well as her big eyes, a worker honeybee has several smaller, simpler light-sensitive organs, ocelli, on her head. These detect approaching dusk, which sends her home to the hive. Her antennae detect odours, temperature, humidity and air vibrations, while the tips of her legs have sensors that detect the nature and concentration of chemicals. Her front legs have a notch she uses to clean her antennae, and her hind legs bear bristles, called a pollen comb, that she uses to pack pollen into the pollen basket.

Listen, then to the buzzing of the bees and respect them. Small they may be, but they know exactly what they're doing.

Bees are undoubtedly busy, but it is the butterflies that people admire more for their splendidly decorated wings. They are also important pollinators, but they don't live in large communities as bees do. When you see them fluttering through the flowers you can be sure it's just the nectar they're after. That's their only food as adults, and their adult lives are brief. They spend most of their lives as larvae – caterpillars – feeding on leaves.

A few species of butterflies and moths don't eat at all as adults, and there are some that eat solid food, but the majority feed on nectar, which they obtain by means of a long proboscis that they keep safely rolled up while they're flying. Well, it would get in the way.

The proboscis is made from two tubes lying side by side. They can be separated for cleaning, but most of the time they're held together by hooks. The insect inserts its proboscis into the nectar secreted at the base of its flower and expands and contracts a sac in its head to suck up the liquid.

Butterflies play a vital role in the life of the flower border. Many plants have flowers with nectar that is inaccessible to the short proboscis of a bee, fly or hoverfly. Butterflies have a much longer reach, which helps the flowers by limiting the species the pollinator visits and thereby increasing the likelihood of productive pollination.

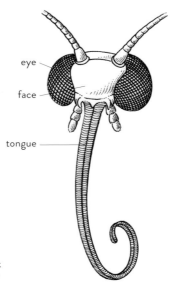

eye

face

tongue

The proboscis, or 'tongue', of a moth. The insect uses it to suck up nectar and keeps it securely rolled up when it's not in use.

What is pollen?
—

They say it's love that makes the world go round, but really it's pollen. Where would any of us be without it? It's no exaggeration to say that all plant and animal life depends on pollen, and that includes you and me. Pollen consists of grains containing the sperm that fertilize the eggs of female flowers, and plants devote a great deal of trouble and energy to ensuring the safe transport of those sperm to their destination. If they didn't, of course, they wouldn't be able to reproduce so they'd die out and we'd have no plants. And if there were no plants what would we eat? Airborne pollen may set you sniffing and sneezing, but the world would be much poorer without it. For one thing, we humans wouldn't exist.

Pollen grains are very delicate. Exposed to the air, they will dry out and die in a matter of hours, and even faster in bright, warm sunshine. It's also the case that pollen grains can survive for thousands of years. Scientists recover fossil pollen from ancient soils and sediments and identify the plants that produced it. And that, you may think, presents us with a paradox. Only it doesn't, because the second statement is a consequence of the first.

Because it's delicate but has to travel from one plant to another, a pollen grain is enclosed in a two-layered case, the thin inner intine and outer exine, and the exine is partly made from one of the toughest and most chemically inert of all biological substances. It's not totally invulnerable to the natural process of decay, but plants produce pollen grains in such vast numbers that at least some of the exines survive.

Most pollen grains are spherical or oval. Those from spruce, pine and fir trees have two or three tiny air-filled sacs to help orient them as they move through the air, for like all conifers, these are wind-pollinated. Pollen grains come in a wide range of sizes. The smallest is that of forget-me-not, which is about 0.005 millimetres across. Melons, at the other end of the scale, produce pollen grains forty times larger, at about 0.2 millimetres.

Scientists are able to link many pollen grains to the plants that produced them, going partly by the grain size, but principally because the grain shrinks as it forms and in pollen that's designed to be carried by animals this bends and twists the surface of the exine into patterns of spines, furrows, and pores. These patterns are characteristic of the plant. Wind-borne pollen is different. Its grains have a thinner coat and are less dense, and their exines are smoother. This makes grasses, for example, more difficult to identify by this method.

Pollen production
—

The production of pollen begins in the anthers, which originate as masses of identical cells. As the flower matures the cells differentiate. Some near the centre of the mass divide twice, so that one cell becomes four, but in such a way that each of the four contains only one set of chromosomes, rather than the two sets found in other cells. These are the sperm cells. The other cells in the anther form the inner wall of the anther itself, and tube-shaped cells that surround the sperm.

These single-celled tubes and their contents are pollen grains. In flowering plants each pollen grain consists of three cells: the tube cell containing its own cell nucleus, and two sperm cells, and these three cells are enclosed in an inner wall, the intine, and an outer wall, the exine. The pores in the exine are where the coat is thinner than elsewhere. If the pollen grain lands on and sticks to, or is caught by, a stigma, its pollen tube will grow through one of the exine pores and into the style of the female flower.

Fully formed and ripe, the pollen is now ready to go. If it's to disperse on the wind it will have to wait for the moving air to bear it away. Wind-borne pollen grains are small, between 0.002 and 0.006 millimetres in size, and their lack of external sculpture means they don't stick together. They drift on the wind until the feathery device on the top of a compatible stigma catches them. Or until they disappear up someone's nose.

Being small and light, airborne pollen grains travel singly and there's not much to them. They're hardly worth eating, even if there were an animal able to catch them in flight, which there isn't. But before they leave, while the grains are all together, there are a few insects that eat them. In the case of one bamboo species, which is a grass, the insects visiting the male flowers have been observed to feed exclusively on the pollen. It's possible that in doing so some of the pollen might have clung to them, but they were so ill-mannered as to ignore the female flowers completely, so this was no help to the plant.

It's always possible that airborne pollen grains may collide with an insect before reaching another plant, and that may be why insects sometimes turn up with grass pollen on their bodies. Insects often carry a static electric charge, so another possibility is that pollen grains are drawn to them as they fly through a pollen cloud.

Insects pollinated the earliest flowering plants. That's how it all began. But there are some places where insects are few and far between. To deal with that, plants took to bearing hermaphrodite flowers and pollinating themselves. Wind pollination was an alternative, however, once plants managed to produce pollen that didn't clump together.

There's just one more problem the plants face. Lots of animals eat pollen. Even people are getting in on it. You can buy pollen marketed as a dietary supplement or even as a food, as though you could order a plate of pollen and chips. It's mostly carbohydrate, of course, with up to about 35 per cent protein, but you'd need to eat a lot of it to meet your daily nutritional requirements.

Pollinia

—

Bees and other pollinating insects gather lumps of stuck-together pollen, but many species of orchids and milkweeds – up to about 25,000 plant species in all – have found a way to help. It's not really the insects they're helping, of course, but themselves. Their aim is to make sure the visitors go away with the heaviest load of pollen they can pile on to them, and the way to do that is to work on the stickiness aspect of the grains. Different plants go about this in different ways, so there are a few variations on a central theme. The theme is that the flower packages its pollen grains stuck together in bundles, rather than producing unpredictably varying numbers of separate pollen grains. These pollen parcels are called pollinia.

Each pollinium has an exterior sticky projection, shaped and oriented in such a way that it sticks to a visiting insect, usually a moth or butterfly. The insect flies off with it to the next plant, where the pollinium catches in a groove in the stigma, from where its pollen grains fertilize the flower; and one of that flower's pollinia sticks to the insect, to be carried to the next flower. It's a system that fascinated Charles Darwin, who described it in 1862 in *On the Various Contrivances by which British and Foreign Orchids are Fertilised by Insects, and on the Good Effects of Intercrossing.*

Two pollinia of *O. mascula* on the sharpened tips of pencils. A shows the pollinia when first attached and B shows it after the act of depression. These drawings by Charles Darwin appeared in *On the Various Contrivances by which British and Foreign Orchids are Fertilised by Insects, and on the Good Effects of Intercrossing.* (John Murray, London, 1862).

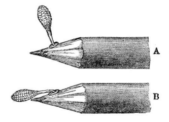

You can quite understand that pollinia save everyone a whole lot of bother. The plant guarantees that the visiting insect picks up a good cargo of pollen grains in return for its nectar high, and the insect is not in the least inconvenienced. Some pollinia are hard, some soft, and they may be club-shaped or flattened. In many plants they occur in pairs joined together.

Look carefully and pollinia are big enough to see. You'll need a powerful microscope to see a single pollen grain, but as Darwin's drawings of pollinia on the tips of sharpened pencils show, orchid pollinia are quite large.

Buzz pollination
—

All of this assumes that the ripe anthers split open longitudinally to expose the sticky lumps of pollen inside. But a small number of plants don't work that way. Determined to make life difficult, for themselves as much as for the insects you might think, their anthers are tubes, sealed except for a tiny pore at the tip. Confronted with anthers of this type, a would-be pollinator may be flummoxed. It's clearly an anther, so there must be pollen inside, but how can it get at it? And to make matters worse, plants with tubular anthers don't produce nectar, so it's pollen or nothing for the insect.

Halictid bee vibrating her wings to detach pollen from the anthers of a pale meadow beauty flower (*Rhexia mariana*)

The first time it encounters such an anther an insect has no idea what to do about it. It will spend a considerable time exploring the flower until the penny finally drops. What you need to do is position yourself correctly then buzz your wings just as fast as you can. The buzzing generates a strong force – scientists have measured it at 30g, which would kill a person exposed to it for more than a few seconds. That force drives the pollen out through the pore at the tip of the anther. It's called buzz pollination.

Of course, it's only bees that can buzz their wings fast enough to make this work, but oddly enough most honeybees don't do it. Many bumblebees have acquired the knack, as have a variety of smaller bees. The one in the picture is a sweat bee (family Halictidae), somewhat smaller than a honeybee.

Perfumes
—

If you're a male plant you don't want to waste any more pollen than you have to. It's important stuff, after all. The trouble is, from your point of view, pollinating insects, birds, bats, and all the rest of them, including giraffes and monkeys, are pretty stupid. They won't hesitate to help themselves to your pollen, but you've absolutely no guarantee that they'll deposit even a smidgeon of it on an empathic female's stigma. All they're interested in is a free lunch and as for romance, so far as you can tell they wouldn't have the remotest idea what the word means. So, being smarter than most people give them credit for, the plants do something about it.

Clearly, the pollinators must be taught that there's no such thing as a free lunch. How do you teach them? It's fairly simple. First, you design your flowers to make them appealing to particular pollinators. Make them bright red, orange or white, for instance, and birds will notice them. Yellow, blue, white or ultraviolet will attract bees, and they'll appreciate a guide to help them find your nectar, brushing against the anthers on their way in, naturally. Purple, pink or white flowers will attract moths, butterflies like red and purple and they also follow nectar guides. Purple, green or white flowers will attract bats, and in their case you can close your flowers by day to reduce wear and tear. And so it goes, colours designed for pollinators. You should also adjust the shape of the flower. A narrow tube with a wide platform for perching on will suit a butterfly perfectly. Bees also like a landing platform, but the flower needs to be shallower than one designed for butterflies, to allow for their shorter proboscis. You then adapt the amount and type of your pollen, whether or not you supply nectar and how much, and whether or not you emit a perfume, and of what kind.

When you've done all this, with a bit of luck you'll attract a particular type of pollinator and over many generations your special pollinator will get used to you and adapt its own body to the goodies you offer. You'll specialize together, with the result that your pollinator will spend most of its time visiting flowers just like yours. It minimizes the waste of pollen, while at the same time reducing competition among the pollinators.

This is called the pollination syndrome and we can use it to predict the kind of pollinator that will service a particular type of flower. At least, up to a point we can. Nothing in nature is perfect, so it's by no means a strictly one-for-one relationship. There are many exceptions.

Odour may be the most important of all the signals plants use, because flying insects have a sense of smell that makes a bloodhound seem positively anosmic (the posh word for those who lack a sense of smell). A male moth can detect the perfume, called a pheromone, given off by a lone female at a distance of several kilometres.

It didn't start out that way for the insects. They're descended from an ancestor they share with the crustaceans – the lobsters, crabs, shrimps, barnacles, woodlice and their kin – and crustaceans have no sense of smell. So presumably the first insects didn't have one, either, and primitive, nonflying insects such as bristletails lack odour receptors. Insects are believed to have acquired their sense of smell when they took to the air. That's when it started to matter. Flying insects use their sense of smell to locate mates, food, and egg-laying sites.

"Insects are believed to have acquired their sense of smell when they took to the air."

Our sense of smell is poor and that makes it difficult for us to imagine what the world is like to animals that rely on scent the way we rely on sight. As we move around we navigate a landscape of objects, with distinct shapes, colours, and textures that we see. As they fly, insects move through clouds of intermingled smells. There are odours of plants, their flowers, animals, potential mates, decomposing matter, and countless other sources. The odours are emitted as gases, rising into the air like clouds of smoke from a nineteenth-century city's worth of factory chimneys, and as the plumes rise and spread they also mingle. The tiny insect has to be able to sort out this complex mixture to identify the chemical that might mean something just as you or I might recognize the friend alighting from a distant bus on to a crowded street. Compared with this, conducting a quiet conversation in a roomful of loudly chattering partygoers is nothing. But the honeybees, butterflies and all the others manage just fine, and scientists have even trained honeybees to distinguish particular smells.

While we're on the subject, we shouldn't forget that plants have a sense of smell, too. Plant parasites, such as dodder, locate their hosts by detecting the chemicals they emit by means of their odour; when a herbivore attacks a plant the victim starts secreting chemical repellents and emits odours that nearby plants detect so that they can start secreting their own herbivore deterrents.

Perfumes are very important attractants, and not only to pollinators. People have been cultivating plants for their perfumes for thousands of years and some of those perfumes have great cultural resonance. Not all of them are flower perfumes, however. Frankincense, certainly one of the most famous, is a resin obtained by cutting through the bark of a tree and waiting for the sap that oozes from the cut to set hard. Several species of *Boswellia* supply frankincense, the best quality coming from *B. sacra*. Myrrh is also a resin, obtained in the same way as frankincense, but from species of *Commiphora*, which are small, thorny trees related to *Boswellia*.

There are about 25 species of mint (*Mentha*) and hundreds of hybrids and varieties. Again, it's not the flowers that release their strong perfume, but in this case the leaves and stems. The flowers provide nectar for the bees that pollinate them and unlike most flowers they perform an additional service, for the menthol they secrete kills the parasitic mites on their bee visitors. Their menthol also deters herbivorous insects. People, on the other hand, love it and have done so for centuries.

The rose, cherished and cultivated for at least five thousand years, sacred to Isis and Aphrodite, has been adopted as a symbol many times by many parties. In medieval England the Wars of the Roses were fought between the houses of Lancaster, with the symbol of the red *Rosa gallica*, and York, which adopted the white *R. alba*. It has other, less obvious connotations. A confidential communication is sometimes said to be sub rosa, under the rose, because the Romans used to place a rose outside a room in which secret discussions were taking place. No one does that any more, but it's surprising how long the memory of traditions can survive.

Boswellia sacra, the tree that supplies most of the world's frankincense.

Boswellia Carterii Birdw.

Rosa gallica

(Vulgaris ochracea marginata)

P. J. Redouté pinx.   Imprimerie de Rémond

Rosa gallica, the Gallic or French rose, is also the red rose
of Lancaster. One variety is known as the apothecary's rose
as it was grown for its medicinal properties over many centuries.

Jasmine (*Jasminum*) is especially fragrant – indeed, its name is a transliteration of the Arabic word for 'fragrant flower'. Butterflies and moths are hard pushed to pollinate its flowers before people pick them to make perfumed garlands. It's of Asian origin but cultivated in most parts of the world.

Lavender (*Lavandula*) is a kind of northern equivalent to jasmine, widely grown for its perfumed flowers. There are about 39 species, related to the mints, and nations seem keen to claim their own: there's English lavender, French lavender, Spanish lavender, Egyptian lavender and possibly more. Lavender's popularity is such that it is grown commercially as a field crop, pollinated by bees.

Orchids are among the most successful of plants, for there are more than 22,000 species of them and they grow in almost every part of the world. Most have attractive flowers, many of them perfumed. They use every trick in the book and a few they invented for themselves to attract the insects that pollinate them. Many supply nectar, but they also use the fragrance, colour and shape of their flowers, with the result that for them the pollination syndrome is taken almost to extremes, so closely are the flowers and their pollinators adapted to each other.

This extreme specialization is one of the many attractions orchids have for growers. Since it is only a particular insect that can pollinate a particular orchid flower, the flower has to be prepared to wait a long time for a pollinator to chance by. In other words, once the flower opens it must remain so and can sit waiting patiently on the sideboard for ages. Indeed, plonked down in the sitting room rather than the big wide world that is its home, the poor old flower could wait forever. It can't manage that, of course, but it will remain ornamental for longer than most flowers.

One of the most unusual arrangements in the plant world has developed between a large group of tropical New World orchids and the bees that pollinate them. These orchids produce no nectar and each flower hides its pollen in pollinia beneath a cap on its single anther. Male bees – never females – have large brushes on their front legs that they use to extract

Labiat

Lavandula vera D.C.

W.Müller n.d. Nat.

certain volatile chemicals from the flower and the pollinia stick to the bee as it passes. The bee, indifferent to the pollinia of course, transfers the chemicals to combs on its middle legs and uses these to pack them into grooves on its hind legs. The orchid has given the bee nothing at all to eat, but that's not what this is about. As the bee flies off, the volatile chemicals in its leg grooves gradually vaporize and waft through the forest air to where, so hopes Mister Bee, the antennae of an interested female bee will detect them. Miss Bee flies up the chemical gradient, the two meet, love blooms, and in due course the world is blessed with a new generation of bees. They're called orchid bees, for obvious reasons, and many of them are a bright metallic green. Charles Darwin was one of the first naturalists to describe these orchids and their bees, but he mistakenly thought the orchid bees were female.

LEFT: Lavender (*Lavandula angustifolia*) is grown extensively for its perfume. ABOVE: The green orchid bee (*Euglossa dilemma*) specializes in pollinating particular species of orchids in return for the flower's fragrant secretions. This is a male bee.

And pongs

—

When you think about it, there must be quite a bit of competition for pollinators. Busy as they are, bees can't be everywhere, and while I'm sure the butterflies and moths do their best, they don't fly all that fast so there must be a limit to the number of flowers each individual is able to visit in the course of a working day. So, if you're a plant, what's the best thing to do? Well, you could spread your net wider, as it were, and try attracting other kinds of animals. Anything will do, after all, provided it's mobile.

As you know, while we may consider particular flowers pretty, prettiness is irrelevant to a plant's success. What matters is whether the flowers catch the eye of a certain pollinating insect. And the same, obviously, goes for perfume. A rose by any other name might smell as sweet, but the fact that poets and lovers find it romantic is neither here nor there. What do the bees make of it?

If the bees are too busy and you're unable to make a perfume more gorgeous than a rose, maybe you should go for something entirely different. As well as the bees and butterflies there are lots of flies, and those that feed on rotting meat are used to travelling long distances in search of a meal. They have to because you don't find dead bodies lying around all over the place, do you? So why not try producing a flower that smells like rotting meat? And just to make sure, you'd better make it a big flower, so it puts out a lot of perfume and the flies have no excuse for not finding it.

Once a plant sets its mind to it, there's no end to what it can achieve. In its enthusiasm for carrion flies, the titan arum (*Amorphophallus titanum*) has produced one of the world's biggest flowers. It's a spadix three metres (ten feet) tall wrapped in a spathe that's green on the outside and dark red on the inside, so when it opens it looks like red meat as well as

The titan arum (*Amorphophallus titanum*)
has a spathe more than three metres (ten feet)
tall, so it's much taller than a man. It smells
of rotting flesh.

smelling of it. Also, it's warm, at about the body temperature of a mammal. The spadix is an inflorescence with both male and female florets, the females opening first and the males a day or two later. When the inflorescence dies the plant produces a single leaf that grows upwards to a height of about six metres (twenty feet) and width of about five metres (sixteen feet). It's quite a plant, and sweat bees, carrion flies and beetles hurry to it from far and wide. The warmth of the spadix helps to disperse the perfume, which is strongest in the middle of the night, when its pollinators are about their business; they can detect it from hundreds of metres away. Once inside, the insects are temporarily trapped. On arrival they deliver any pollen they're carrying, then they have to wait until the female flowers have ceased to be receptive and the male flowers are open, so they collect more pollen as they leave. The flower usually opens in the afternoon and remains open all night, after which it dies.

The titan arum – the name given to it by Sir David Attenborough – grows naturally only in Sumatra, although many botanic gardens cultivate it for its novelty. It's sometimes called the corpse flower, but that name also belongs to another native of the rainforests of Sumatra and Borneo, *Rafflesia arnoldii* – and it earns the name for the same reason. Awful doesn't begin to describe its smell.

Rafflesia arnoldii has another claim to fame, in producing the world's largest single flower, at up to one metre (about a yard) across and weighing up to ten kilograms (twenty-two pounds). The plant is a parasite, lacking leaves, stems, and roots, and its flower is the only part anyone ever sees. The rest of the plant spends several years inside its host's stems and roots in the form of thin strands winding their way around and absorbing nutrients, until it erupts through the bark as a small bud, which takes about nine months to mature. Then it opens its five reddish-brown petals with orange spots. The flower lasts for up to a week or so and then it's gone. The flower is either male or female, and is pollinated by carrion flies – bluebottles. The plant produces several litres of foul-smelling nectar, but despite its best efforts pollination doesn't happen very often because the plant is extremely rare and individuals are widely scattered. Not surprisingly, perhaps, having failed to get its reproduction properly organized, the plant is endangered.

Up to one metre (about a yard) across, the corpse flower (*Rafflesia arnoldii*) is the world's largest individual flower. The plant itself is a parasite.

Jackal food (*Hydnora africana*) is another parasite, in this case of the roots of euphorbias. A native of southern Africa, it has no leaves or stem and only the top of its flower projects above the ground, growing directly from the root. Its top part is tubular with three thick structures, united at the top but open below and orange on the inside, in an arrangement that in a more orthodox plant might be called sepals. The flower smells strongly of faeces and attracts dung beetles, which clamber inside and remain trapped until they've pollinated it. The plant doesn't expect the beetles to work for nothing. It provides them with a special edible tissue and doesn't mind them eating some of its pollen and cells of the stigmas.

There are also stinky arums and some of them grow closer to home. The western or yellow skunk cabbage is one. It's an American plant and named by folk who know what a skunk can do if you insult it, but it's cultivated quite extensively in other parts of the world for its spectacular yellow spathe and spadix and its huge leaves, more than one metre (about a yard) long. Flies and beetles pollinate it. It can be invasive where it has been introduced, but it's popular. It grows in wet soil, but don't grow it too near the house or you'll wish you hadn't.

The snake lily grows in the Balkans and eastern Mediterranean region. It's another arum, this time with a purple spadix and spathe. Its long spadix strikes some people as resembling a dragon inside the spathe, hence the name, though I can't see it myself. Among other names, it's also called the voodoo lily and stink lily. When it flowers the blowflies are drawn helplessly to its delicious aroma of rotting meat.

The red inside of the titan arum's spathe is vaguely reminiscent of meat, but the aptly named dead horse arum tries harder. Its red spathe divides in two and between them the spadix is covered in what look like hairs. The result bears a passing resemblance to the rear end of a dead horse complete with tail, and it's irresistible to blowflies. Female flies arrive seeking a place to lay their eggs, and scramble around the spathe, depositing pollen they collected from other flowers on to the receptive stigmas. But when they try to leave they find themselves trapped and have to remain inside the flower overnight. In the morning, the anthers are mature and the stigmas no longer receptive, so as they depart the flies collect more pollen, which they carry to the next plant.

What's more, like the titan arum, the dead horse arum (*Helicodiceros muscivorus*) is one of the few plants that can raise its temperature, which makes the scent from its 'tail' travel farther. The plant grows naturally in the Mediterranean region. So far as I know, no one grows this plant for pleasure or ornament.

People do cultivate the giant starfish flower (*Stapelia gigantea*), a succulent perennial that looks like a cactus but isn't. It belongs to the milkweed family and comes from tropical and southern Africa. When it flowers, its five fleshy lobes, up to forty centimetres (sixteen inches) across, make it look rather like a starfish. The flowers seldom last longer than two days, but the plant produces a succession of them. It's another plant you don't want to grow too close to the house, because the flowers smell strongly of rotting meat, giving the plant its other name of carrion flower.

There's even an orchid that smells of carrion. It's called *Bulbophyllum phalaenopsis* and grows naturally in Indonesia. Only dedicated orchid fanciers grow it, so I guess it doesn't need a common name. It's a big plant that grows from a pseudobulb up to fifteen centimetres (six inches) across, with a leathery leaf up to one metre (about a yard) long and thirty centimetres (twelve inches) wide. The inflorescences consist of up to twenty flowers, each up to eight centimetres (three inches) long.

Attracting the birds

—

If you (I'm still seeing things from the plant's point of view here), can't persuade even the dung beetles and bluebottles to give you so much as a passing glance, maybe it's time to try the birds. There are lots of them, they're all over the place and they're highly mobile, so how difficult can it be?

If you live in the Americas, a hummingbird would be a good choice. The brownbreast, also known as the rufous-breasted hermit or hairy hermit, is a bird about ten centimetres (four inches) long that lives in Central America and on some of the Caribbean islands, and it's quite common. Brownbreasts have long bills that are ideal for supping nectar from tubular flowers. They may not be entirely suitable, however, because unfortunately they're very choosy, taking an interest only in flowers that precisely match the length of their bill, and seldom bothering with flowers that are more than five meters (sixteen feet) above ground. Heliconias are their favourites. The bird approaches the flower from slightly above, thrusts downward with its bill, then lets its body sink to below the top of the flower. This allows its curved bill to penetrate all the way to the nectar. The flower has sticky threads that help attach pollen to the bird's bill. Sometimes brownbreasts also use their tongues to capture insects from the underside of leaves.

Heliconias are red, a colour which birds are attracted to; most bird-pollinated flowers opt for one or other shade of this colour. Happily, not all hummingbirds are as fussy as the brownbreast, and a flower that attracts one species will likely attract others. Many hummingbird species love the autumn sage (*Salvia greggii*), for instance, which flowers in summer despite its name. The plant is native to the southern United States and Mexico, but it's widely cultivated in other parts of the world, with cultivars in a variety of colours. In the wild, though, its flowers are red.

The brownbreast, rufous-breasted hermit, or hairy hermit (*Glaucis hirsutus*), formerly known as the mazeppa, is a hummingbird that lives in Central America and the Caribbean. It feeds on nectar augmented by insects.

Desert willow (*Chilopsis linearis*) comes from the same part of the world as autumn sage. It isn't a willow at all but a member of the bignonia family, making it a relative of jacaranda, though the leaves resemble those of willow. The desert willow is generous with its nectar, which attracts carpenter bees, bumblebees and butterflies, as well as hummingbirds and other birds.

Fairy duster (*Calliandra eriophylla*), a low-growing, evergreen shrub belonging to the pea and bean family, is another plant from that area, its name referring to the many long pink stamens that protrude from its pink flowers. Its nectar attracts flies, bees, butterflies and hummingbirds. It doesn't need much water, which allows it to thrive where thirstier plants can't, including in the Mojave Desert. That's its strength, but the fairy duster is being too clever by half, because it stands out alone in the desert and many animals, including deer, find it deliciously tasty. There's not much point stealing a march on your competitors if you're simply setting yourself up as a deer's dinner.

Penstemons are popular garden plants and there are many species, some pollinated by bumblebees and others by hummingbirds. From the plant's point of view, the latter seem the better option. That's because bumblebees collect pollen to feed their larvae, and although the anthers dust the bees fairly thoroughly, the bees groom themselves meticulously, gathering up almost all the pollen and packing it into their pollen sacs. Obviously, the bees aren't deliberately going to deposit any of the pollen from their pollen sacs on the stigma of the next flower they visit, which makes them somewhat inefficient pollinators for this plant, compared with hummingbirds. They're there for the nectar and have not the slightest interest in pollen. Pollen that sticks to a bird's bill is very likely to reach the stigma of the next flower.

It seems likely that in the distant past all the penstemons were bee-pollinated and that over the generations some of them have modified their flowers to make them less accessible to bees and more attractive to hummingbirds. So, you see, with patience and persistence it is possible to change. You could do better.

What do you do, though, if people cart you to the other side of the ocean, far away from the hummingbirds with which you had such a special relationship? That's what happened to the fuchsias. They originated in South America, but gardeners fell heavily for them and now you find them everywhere in Europe. They've escaped from cultivation and grow in hedgerows. They're almost weeds in some places, and meanwhile all the hummingbirds are imprisoned in zoos. The answer, of course, is to widen your horizons. Bees and other insects have moved in and the fuchsias have had to make do. And they're doing just fine.

Bees can be very pushy, but then they rely on nectar and pollen and can't easily find alternatives. At one time there were no honeybees in Australia and vertebrate animals, especially birds known as honeyeaters, were the usual pollinators. Once the honeybees arrived, however, starting in the 1820s, they began to take over and today bees and honeyeaters compete. The change sometimes affects the quality of the plant's seeds. Studies of *Callistemon citrinus*, one of the fifty species of bottlebrushes, all of which are native to Australia and used to be pollinated by honeyeaters, found that seeds from plants pollinated by both honeyeaters and honeybees germinated faster than those from plants pollinated solely by honeybees.

The common red bottlebrush (*Callistemon citrinus*), native to Australia, is pollinated by bees, birds and even geckos.

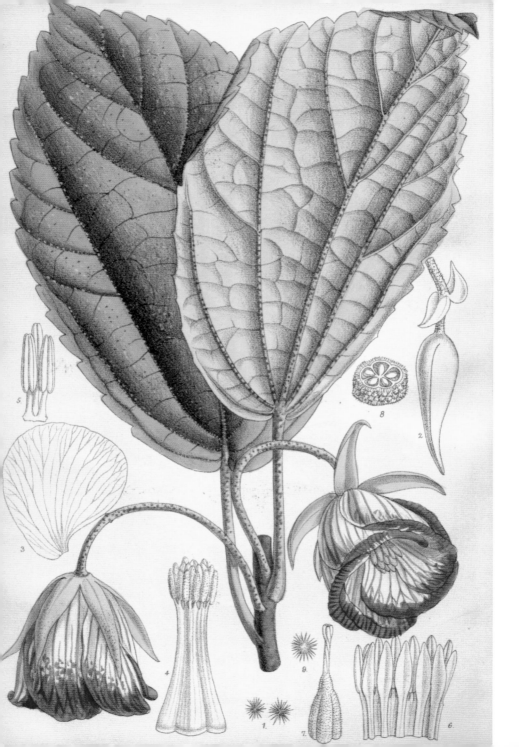

Bottlebrushes aren't too particular about their visitors, mind. It seems anyone is welcome, including geckos. But there's one plant that specializes in gecko-pollination. *Trochetia* – there is no common name – is a genus of six species of shrubs and small trees, with five species occurring only on Mauritius and one on La Réunion. They're unusual in producing red nectar. No one knows just why trochetias do this, but the geckos that pollinate them seem to prefer their nectar coloured. Nor does anyone know whether the birds that also pollinate these flowers find red nectar attractive.

The flowers are red, pink, orange or white, and they're hermaphrodite. Their pollinating bird is the Mauritius white-eye, olive-green and about the size of a sparrow, with a white ring around each eye. The geckos belong to the genus *Phelsuma*, the one visiting the flowers most often being *P. cepediana*, the blue-tailed day gecko; while most geckos are nocturnal, *Phelsuma* species are active by day, hence the common name. They spend most of their time in trees and shrubs and often visit suburban gardens.

LEFT: *Trochetia blackburniana* grows in the Mascarene Islands and is pollinated by a gecko. ABOVE: The blue-tailed day gecko (*Phelsuma cepediana*) is the lizard most often seen pollinating *Trochetia blackburniana*.

If it's birds you fancy as pollinators, there's one final trick you might consider, just to make sure your visitors don't cheat on you by grabbing the snack while missing the pollen. *Axinaea* plants, which live in the American tropics, have found their own answer. Their flowers occur singly or in clusters of up to twenty, and they've modified their stamens so each one ends in a prominent bulb. The bulbs are red, as are the petals, and highly nutritious. Birds are attracted to them, but when a bird tugs at one to remove it, air in the tissue of the stamen is forced under pressure into the anther, which is hollow, causing a jet of air carrying a cloud of pollen grains to issue from the tip of the anther and blast directly into the bird's face. The bird gets pollen all over its head, but it also gets the tasty food item. The blast of pollen is no more than a minor inconvenience, if that, so the rewarded bird returns again and again. And it's not just one bird. Several species of tanagers and finches are regular customers.

Most flowers offer refreshment in return for being pollinated, but not all of them by any means, and other inducements are possible. If your flowers are the right shape you can offer them as meeting places, like clubrooms. Ragworts do this. They belong to the aster family and bear clusters of flower heads. Look closely at these in summer – but not so closely that you scare the members away – and you're likely to see quite large numbers of insects of different species, all mingling together sociably as they wander across the flowers. It's a sort of working insects' club, and it's nice to see them all getting along so well.

N.600.

a. Jacobæa vulgaris major, Jacobæe.
b. Jacobæa vulgaris laciniata flo-
ribus albicantibus.

Common ragwort (*Senecio jacobaea*) on the left is a biennial that can become perennial if it's cut down repeatedly. Poisonous to mammals, insects love it and more than 100 species visit it, some of them very rare. Flies, moths, butterflies, and bees pollinate its flowers and one plant can produce more than 2000 seeds.

CHAPTER 6

APHRODISIACS

Enough of plants and their nuptuals, now let's
have a look at what plants can do for us.

Plants
for lovers
—

'There's rosemary, that's for remembrance; pray, love, remember; and there is pansies, that's for thoughts. . . .

'There's fennel for you, and columbines: — there's rue for you; and here's some for me: — we may call it herb-grace o' Sundays: — O, you must wear your rue with a difference. — There's a daisy; — I would give you some violets, but they withered all when my father died ...'

So said Ophelia (*Hamlet*, Act IV Scene V). Most flowering plants, perhaps all, have cultural meanings and we value many for more than food. In producing poisons to protect themselves against herbivores, for instance, many plants produce chemical substances from which we derive medicines. It's also true that in some cases such values are exaggerated or imaginary, based on the doctrine of signatures, an idea that sprang up in many parts of the world. This held that God had provided clues to help us identify the plants that would cure our ailments. These clues might refer to the colour and taste of the plant – red and bitter plants were good for the heart, black and salty ones for the lungs, green and sour ones for the liver, and so on. Others referred to the overall appearance of the plant, and this often gave it a common name. Liverwort is good for the liver, eyebright for the eyes, lungwort for the respiratory system, snakeroot for snakebites, wormwood for intestinal parasites, and there were many more, all based on the mistaken idea that like cures like.

And mandrake, with a root supposedly resembling a man, would increase sexual desire in women.

Now, to country folk of old that's not such a daft idea. They knew, as we know, that flowers are sexual organs and their only purpose in blooming is to attract love partners, however brief the encounter. Indeed, Linnaeus, the great Swedish botanist who classified thousands of plants and animals, giving them Latin names which in many cases scientists still use, based his entire plant classification system on the arrangement of their stamens and pistils – their sex organs. When he was twenty-three he wrote of them as 'husbands' and 'wives', occupying

'... bridal beds which the Creator has so gloriously arranged, adorned with such noble bed curtains, and perfumed with so many soft scents that the bridegroom with his bride might there celebrate their nuptials with so much the greater solemnity.'

(*Praeludia Sponsaliorum Plantarum*
[On the prelude to the wedding of plants], 1729)

Let us, then, turn aside for a moment from considering how the plants arrange their nuptials and ask not what the plants can do for each other, but rather what the plants can do for us. Which are the plants credited with aphrodisiac properties?

Orchids are where the doctrine of signatures meets Aphrodite, making that a good place to begin. *Orkhis* is the Greek word for testicle and 'orchid' is derived from it. That's a promising start. The reason becomes evident when you see the tubers that certain species, but not all, produce to store nutrients. They do resemble testicles and that's how the family acquired the name Orchidaceae. Apparently this wasn't shortened to 'orchid' until the last century, when John Lindley, the eminent botanist and authority on these plants, used the word in, of all things, a school botany. You'd think he'd have known better, but the book, first published in 1839, went through twelve editions, so perhaps no one noticed.

Naturally, I wouldn't expect you to fall for something so apparently based on false principles, but here's an odd

The milky orchid (*Neotinia lactea*, formerly *Orchis acuminata*), native to
southern Europe, is one of the species whose tubers were ground into
a flour and used to make salep, a drink with supposed aphrodisiac properties.

thing. *Vanda tessellata* is an orchid that lives as an epiphyte throughout the Indian subcontinent, and its flowers have many medicinal uses. A few years ago researchers discovered that the flowers produce a substance with the catchy name of 2,7,7-tri methyl bicyclo [2.2.1] heptane. If a man drinks an infusion of the flowers, within half an hour this compound will increase levels of nitric oxide in his penis, and the nitric oxide will increase levels of another compound that causes vasodilation, thereby causing penile erection. Its action is the same as that of sildenafil, better known as Viagra. And it works whether he remembers the magic ingredient is 2,7,7-tri methyl bicyclo [2.2.1] heptane or not.

The lesser periwinkle, a pretty, five-petalled, mauve, woodland flower, has many uses in folk medicine, and perhaps more beside. Nicholas Culpeper, the seventeenth-century English herbalist, wrote, a little ambiguously, that 'Venus owns this herb, and saith, that herbs eaten by Man and Wife together, cause Love between them.' At one time it's said that the hopeful administered love philtres from lesser periwinkle to their beloved.

Coneflowers, a group of about ten *Echinacea* species, are North American plants with many healing properties, especially for coughs and sore throats. They're also said to combat impotence and to act as an aphrodisiac.

You wouldn't think a supper of garlic makes the best preparation for a night of passion, unless you both eat it perhaps, but among the long list of maladies garlic is alleged to address, it is recommended as an aphrodisiac and has been used for this purpose since ancient times and in many parts of the world. Modern evidence is that it may help with various heart and circulation problems and colds, but you'd need to eat quite a lot of it. There may be something in its ability to stimulate sexual desire, however, because in some traditions Buddhist monks and nuns are forbidden to eat garlic because it gives rise to thoughts that distract from meditation. It's said that you can make a love potion from the juices of garlic and coriander.

"Buddhist monks and nuns are forbidden to eat garlic because it gives rise to thoughts that distract from meditation."

On the other hand, at ancient Greek festivals when women sang hymns in praise of Demeter, goddess of harvests, women chewed garlic to deter sexual advances. Or, according to Aristophanes, they chewed garlic in the morning so their husbands, who couldn't imagine any man wanting to sleep with a woman reeking of garlic, wouldn't know what they'd been up to the night before.

'Sing maidens, and mothers sing after them,
"Demeter, greatly welcome, feeder of many,
bringer of many measures."'
(*Hymn to Demeter*)

Of course, everyone knows you should always wear a garlic clove round your neck and smear garlic round the doors and windows if there are vampires or werewolves about. I don't think it works for zombies.

Fenugreek has been employed as a love stimulant at least since the days of ancient Egypt. The Egyptians also used it in embalming, though, so perhaps you should be careful. It's the seeds that you use to make an infusion to drink, and it's also sold in the form of a liquid extract or tincture. It freshens the breath, which helps especially if you've been eating garlic, and fenugreek does contain a long list of medically active ingredients, so maybe there's something in its reputation.

In many cultures the coneflower (*Echinacea purpurea*) is believed to stimulate sexual desire.

Cloves also freshen the breath and relieve toothache. As a sex stimulant they're best when mixed with cinnamon. You either chew them or smear their essential oils on your skin. Alternatively you can add a pinch of ground cloves and cinnamon to your coffee. The spices work by stimulating secretion of testosterone, which increases libido in both men and women.

Basil has also been prized as an aphrodisiac. Its leaves have a strong and very pleasant scent and at one time that scent was believed to drive men insane with desire. If you want to attract your lover, try placing a pot of basil on the windowsill. Obviously, it won't work unless you explain what it's about, in which case it might not be needed. Still, it's said to work by those well read in such matters. And if a woman wants a man to fall in love with her she should offer him a sprig of basil. If he takes it he's hooked. Culpeper believed basil would cure bee and scorpion stings, too.

Yarrow is believed to help with performance if drunk as an infusion or chewed. In the Middle Ages, before brewers turned to hops as a flavouring, yarrow was one of the herbs added to beers and ales. Rosemary and valerian were also used and the resulting brew was called 'gruit'. Yarrow promotes courage and love, they say, and the Navajo people once used it as an aphrodisiac.

Ginseng, which is the root of *Panax quinquefolium* or *P. ginseng*, really does contain a range of compounds that enhance physical performance, including that in the sexual realm. It also promotes vitality more generally and increases resistance to stress. So this one probably does work if you follow the instructions when taking it. Too much can have unpleasant side effects, though.

It is thought that fenugreek (*Trigonella foenum-graecum*) increases sexual appetite in both women and men.

CHAPTER 7

KIDNAPPERS

Find out how pitcher plants attract bee-killing hornets, arum lilies trap owl midges, and water lilies draw scarab beetles into their warm, intoxicating brothels.

Plants that take prisoners
—

As though they didn't have enough problems, beekeepers in Belgium, France, Germany, Italy, Portugal, and Spain now have to protect their hives against *Vespa velutina nigrithorax*, a species of hornets from the Shanghai region that have invaded. The British authorities are on the lookout and promise to destroy the nests of any that cross the Channel.

Slightly smaller than European hornets and with a dark abdomen that makes them easy to identify, these Asian hornets feed their larvae on honeybees. They hang around near the entrance to a beehive and seize returning workers. Locked in mortal combat, the two insects fall to the ground, where the hornet bites off the bee's head, then packages the body into a meal, which it takes back to its own nest. Once its larvae grow up the hornet is harmless, but while they have young to feed a hive of hornets, with an average of four thousand adults, can wipe out entire hives of bees.

Help is at hand, however, albeit somewhat limited. One day while examining his *Sarracenia* plants Romaric Perrecheau, head of the botanic garden at Nantes, discovered one of the plants filled with dead Asian hornets. *Sarracenia* is a genus of American pitcher plants, carnivorous plants with a scent and nectar that the hornets evidently find enticing. They climb over the rim of the pitcher, then slip and fall all the way inside, where juices secreted by the plant digest them.

While their assistance is undoubtedly welcome, the pitcher plants won't be able to control the hornets unaided, but their intervention shows that plants can take advantage of new sources of food. They're aware of their surroundings and adaptable.

Like all arum lilies, cuckoo-pint has an inflorescence consisting of a spadix enclosed by a spathe, and in some people's dirty minds the sexual imagery is obvious. It used to be called priest's-pintle, pintle being a country word for penis, and when this was frowned on by the mealy-mouthed gentry, folk took to calling it cuckoo-pint. Still not satisfied, the gentry tried to persuade the lower orders to call it 'our lord and our lady', patiently explaining that the spathe represented Mary's cloak wrapped around the spadix, representing the infant Jesus. Maybe the working classes didn't understand, because they called it lords-and-ladies, which is a bit different.

The spadix emits a smell of faeces that certain insects find irresistible. It also generates warmth, its temperature often being 15°C (27°F) higher than the air around it. The warmth generates convection currents that carry the odour farther from the plant. Owl midges, also called moth flies, are particularly drawn to this perfume, and they also enjoy the warmth. These very small, hairy flies alight on the spadix, only to find themselves trapped there by a ring of hairs that curve downward. They don't remain trapped for long, but as they struggle to break free they receive a generous dusting of pollen.

The Amazon Basin is one of the world's warmer locations and you could be forgiven for thinking there'd be little need for its inhabitants to turn on the heating, but the Amazon waterlily does exactly that. Since the weather is always warm there must be another reason, and there is. It's all to do with the beetles that pollinate its flowers. The waterlily is very famous, of course. Its circular leaves, floating on the water, can be almost three metres (10 feet) in diameter, and its flowers are more than thirty centimetres (twelve inches) across. Botanic gardens with big ponds in their glasshouses love it, so you shouldn't have to search too far to find one.

I'm sorry to have to tell you, though, that the flowers are nothing more than brothels for scarab beetles and to advertise their facilities they release a sweet scent reminiscent of pineapple. They're also warm. At night, which is when the action takes place, they're 6–9°C (11–16°F) warmer than the air. And the beetles know this. One of the problems you have if you're a beetle is that you need to raise your body temperature

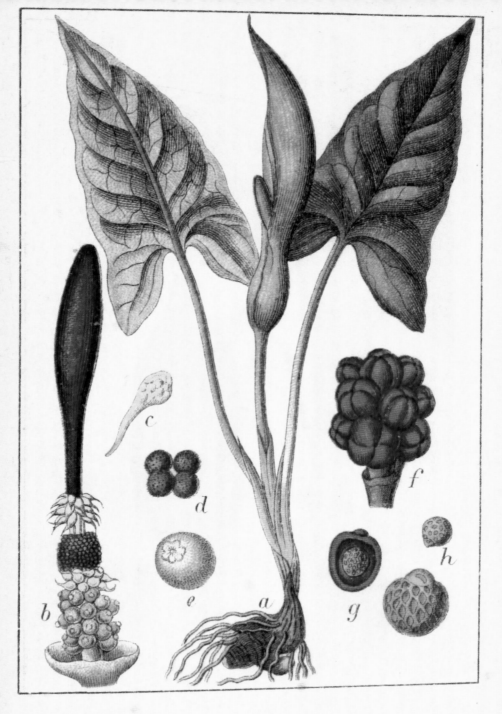

Gemeiner Aronsstab, Arum maculatum.

before you can engage in any vigorous activity. Your muscles literally seize up when they're cold. Now you can get them up to working temperature by doing warm-up exercises, like an athlete, but that consumes energy, which means you'll have to find something to eat to replace it. That's possible, of course, but if a flower exudes warmth it makes obvious sense to take advantage of it. So the beetles, male and female, fly at a leisurely pace to the flowers, looking forward to warming themselves inside, where the flowers also offer refreshment, allowing them to nibble on the styles.

Once inside, the happy trysting beetles negotiate the necessary terms with their newly met partners and all is well. What they fail to notice, or if they do notice it they don't seem to care, is that while they're enjoying their night of passion the flower closes its petals. It keeps the warmth in, of course, but it also shuts the door on the clients. As they move about inside, the beetles deposit any waterlily pollen they may have brought with them on the stigmas around them. That is the price the flowers charge. The lovers usually spend about twenty-four hours in their love nest.

While they're inside and oblivious, the flower changes sex. Its white petals turn pink and the stigmas cease to be receptive. Then the flower opens just a little, forming a narrow tube to the outside, and, passion spent, up the beetles go. As they leave, they have to squeeze past the stamens and anthers, which are now coated in ripe pollen that they smear on the departing guests.

As the example of the hornet-devouring pitcher plants illustrates, some plants are carnivores. Usually they adopt this food source because they inhabit wetlands, bogs and similar places where the soil is very deficient in nutrients, and they've evolved various techniques for catching their insect prey. It would seem sensible, therefore, to approach the task of finding pollinators in much the same way.

Cuckoo-pint, or lords-and-ladies (*Arum maculatum*) is a common plant throughout Europe.

'Since this is what we're good at,' one of them might suggest, 'why don't we simply entice 'em and trap 'em?' Now if this were a strategy meeting among the plants I can hear the immediate objection from down near the bottom of the flower border. 'Hang on. We trap insects to eat them, don't we? OK, we could trick them into pollinating us first, but don't you think the word will get around the insects that their sip of our nectar may be their last? That might put them off, don't you think? And anyway, how are we going to pollinate our mates if we digest the insects we've just dusted with pollen — along with the pollen, for goodness sake? It doesn't make sense.'

Clearly more thought was needed, and after some additional evolutionary planning the carnivores came up with a solution that didn't involve distinguishing between insects that are pollinators and insects that are tea. First, you offer two kinds of reward. You bait your traps with food smells, while offering nectar and pollen to the pollinators. Second, you open your flowers high above the ground and locate your traps much lower down. That way, different types of insects will encounter the flowers and the traps. Finally, and just to make absolutely sure, you open your flowers for pollination at a different time from your food traps – flowers first, traps some time later. And that's how it works and on the whole it works pretty well. Accidents can happen, of course, but it's a rough old world and you have to allow for some collateral damage.

We met orchid bees earlier, and the way they take a really sexy perfume from their favourite orchids. But how do the orchids work? Some people call them bucket orchids, others bat orchids (*Coryanthes* species), and their flowers are peculiar, even for orchids.

The plant produces pseudobulbs, which are swellings on the stems between leaf nodes. Pseudobulbs are used to store nutrients, but in the case of these orchids up to three flowers hang on long stems beneath each swelling. The flowers hang down and as they open, their sepals extend to the sides then bend back, so they look like the wings of a bat, frozen in flight, while another sepal bends down. The petals are tiny and insignificant.

The open flower then has a top part shaped like a helmet, a central part resembling a flume at a swimming pool, and beneath these a deep bucket, which gives the plant its other name.

A sturdy column at the centre, between the 'bat-wing' sepals, has glands that secrete a clear liquid, which drips into the bucket. Male bees seek the perfume because females find it attractive, but the waxy surface of the flower is slippery and they're liable to fall into the bucket. The liquid in the bucket wets their wings, so they're unable to fly, but there is an escape route up a ramp and through an opening so tiny most escaping bees have quite a struggle. Their struggle involves shaking themselves vigorously and their shaking vibrates the anthers bringing down a shower of pollen.

Bucket orchids (*Coryanthes* species, this is *C. albertinae*) depend on orchid bees for pollination, enticing them into their 'buckets', which contain a perfumed liquid that male bees seek because it helps them attract females.

CHAPTER 8

ON THE MAKE-
THE CHEATS

A glimpse inside the villainous world of nectar robbers,
pollen thieves and plant tricksters.

Nectar thieves
—

Think of the word 'criminal' and I bet it conjures an image of a person. Only people can be criminals, after all, because criminality is exclusively human. You can't apply the concept to animals or plants. It wouldn't make sense. Or can you? Sadly, I have to tell you that we live in a world of villainy. It's all around us, in the countryside as in the cities, in our gardens as in the underworld, we live surrounded on all sides by plants and animals of villainous intent. It's not us they're out to deceive, however, but each other. Among the insects crawling, flitting, fluttering and buzzing in and out of the flowers, a significant proportion are rogues, up to no good, on the make. Like their human counterparts, they're cutting corners, taking without giving, taking without the owner's consent. And their rewards? The first one is nectar, the source of a quick burst of energy, the equivalent of a fast buck.

Nectar is sweet and if only we could get flowers to produce more of it, I reckon there'd be a big market and we'd all make our fortunes. You'd be able to buy it in the shops, next to the fizzy drinks. Health foodies would hail it for being natural and the food police would have a great time boosting sales by telling us not to drink it because it would make us fat and rot our teeth (which would encourage us to eat less, you'd think, so we'd lose weight). But flowers produce only tiny amounts, just enough to attract the insects and birds that they then douse with pollen. So there you are. It's all a con and if you fall for it you'll end up dusty.

Unlike people, however, who will fall for almost anything, some birds and insects are canny. Pollen is messy stuff, after all, and who'd want to spend ages trying to clean it off their body or feathers, all for the sake of a quick sugar kick. Much better simply to grab the juice and skip the pollen. And that's a trick many have learned.

About eighteen species of small tropical American birds, aptly called flowerpiercers, specialize in this type of larceny, feeding on nectar from tubular flowers such as fuchsias, honeysuckles, kniphofias (red hot pokers), and penstemons. They have an upper bill that's longer than the lower bill and curved at the tip, and both upper and lower bills have sharp points. A flowerpiercer uses the hook on its upper bill to hold the flower steady, then, mouth wide open, stabs its lower bill through the base of the corolla and into the nectaries, making a hole through which it inserts its long tongue to sup up the sugary prize. And it never comes anywhere near the messy pollen. It doesn't pay for its fix.

The moustached flowerpiercer (this is a subspecies, *Diglossa mystacalis pectoralis*), is a nectar-stealing tanager that lives in Bolivia and Peru.

That, of course, entirely defeats the purpose of having tubular flowers in the first place. They're meant to be so long and narrow that only those pollinating insects or birds with amazingly long tongues can reach the nectar. The floral architecture limits the field, guaranteeing delicious rewards for the long-tongues and persuading them to specialize in similar-looking flowers, which also benefits the plant by reducing greatly the risk that its pollen will end up uselessly in a plant of a different species. Everyone wins. Or did until the crooks turned up.

Many sunbirds perform the same trick. They live in the Old World tropics and in many ways resemble the hummingbirds of the New World, though their aeronautical skills don't extend to flying backwards. These sunbirds also feed on tubular flowers, using their downward-curved bills – both upper and lower mandibles are curved – to pierce the nectaries and rob the flower. There are also thieves in the lands of the hummingbirds across the ocean. Scientists monitored one South American species, the reddish hermit hummingbird (*Phaethornis ruber*), recording the birds visiting ninety-seven species of flowers and stealing nectar from almost thirty per cent of them, mainly from tubular flowers. In fairness, it must be said that they did pollinate most of the flowers they visited, so they weren't full-time miscreants.

Such birds are called nectar robbers and their crimes pay well. But not even they can live on nothing but nectar. Sweet drinks will supply your body with carbohydrate, but you also need protein, and nectar has none. So the nectar-robbing birds also eat insects and spiders, which are good sources of protein. We're also being urged to dine on nutritious deep-fried insects. Once it catches on will there be enough to go round so the birds don't go hungry? You have to wonder.

It's not only birds that inhabit this province of the criminal world. Technically, there's a distinction between those that damage the flowers, which are classed as robbers, and thieves, which are the ones that steal nectar without puncturing the petals or nectaries. Either way it's larceny, and there are also insects that buzz around on the dark side. Don't believe everything you read about the busy bees. Some of the benign border buzzers are busy breaking and burgling.

Carpenter bees, about 500 *Xylocopa* species, are close relatives of honeybees, but bigger, about three centimetres (one inch) long, so they're more the size of bumblebees, and that's their problem. They're too big to climb inside flowers to reach the nectar. So, rather than go hungry (and dieting wouldn't work), they punch into the flower at the base. That leaves a hole, which may catch the eye of a passing honeybee, butterfly, or other insect that ordinarily behaves as an honest, law-abiding pollinator, but perhaps significantly, lacks the apparatus for drilling holes in petals. This sly opportunist sees the hole and enjoys a free meal of the quickly replenished nectar, thereby becoming a secondary thief that profits from the work of the primary robber.

If you see a bee that looks like a bumblebee but is blue, black, or black with a small splash of yellow, it may well be a carpenter bee. In California you might encounter what looks like a golden-yellow bumblebee with green eyes. That's a male (females are metallic black) valley carpenter bee (*Xylocopa varipuncta*). They're called carpenter bees because they bore holes into wood to make their nests, although they don't eat the wood, using it only for construction. They're solitary in that they don't live in colonies like honeybees, but nevertheless they're fairly social.

Many bumblebees (*Bombus* species) also tour gardens looking for flowers to rob. Different species seem to have their own preferences, but they've been caught stealing nectar from delphiniums, aconites, aquilegias, corydalis, orange jewelweed (*Impatiens capensis*), bleeding heart (*Dicentra spectabilis*), and many more. Nectar-robbing bumblebees have modified jaws that help them drill into their target flowers.

Stingless bees, too, are close relatives of honeybees and, like them, produce honey. As their name suggests, they have very short and ineffectual stingers, a feature that makes them harmless to the likes of us and therefore popular with beekeepers and as pets – although they can bite if sorely provoked. But not all of them are paragons. Those of the genus *Trigona* and also a species called *Parapartomona zonata*, all of which live in the New World tropics, have modified jaws similar to those of nectar-robbing bumblebees and they're full-time professional nectar robbers, invading a wide range of flowers. As if that weren't bad enough, some of them are thugs that mug honest pollinators going about their lawful business. And the consequences of their shameful behaviour don't end there. The holes they make provide access to hummingbirds and insects such as ants, bugs, and other bees including other stingless bees, that arrive as secondary thieves to steal nectar. Between them the primary and secondary thieves can rob flowers of just about all their nectar.

Some tropical flowers also produce resin, probably to attract pollinators. It's not quite like the resin coniferous trees produce in that it's slow to harden, which means bees can shape it to line their nests. Floral resin strengthens and waterproofs the nest, and keeps out ants, which avoid it because their feet stick to it. Resin also contains antibacterial, antifungal, and antiviral ingredients, so it helps keep out disease. All stingless bees as well as some honeybees and orchard bees (Euglossini) rob flowers of their resin. Most orchard bees are solitary. They live in Central and South America, apart from one species that has established itself in North America. They're gorgeously coloured in metallic green, blue or gold, but don't be fooled. The tribe includes resin thieves and also parasites that lay their eggs in the nests of other bee species that are tricked into raising the imposters' larvae.

Pollen thieves
—

It's not only nectar and resin that attract thieves – so does pollen. It is rich in proteins and vitamins, so it's worth stealing, and it's difficult for plants to defend it. After all, they need pollinators to take it and once it's gone they've lost control of it. They have no guarantee of the honesty of their visitors.

Some of the plants that rely on buzz pollination take out insurance; the size of their flowers restricts the insects that can gain access. This ensures that the big fat bee that buzzes out the pollen can't help bumping against the stigma of the next flower it visits, and most buzz pollinators are indeed big and busy, not spending long in each flower before moving on to call on many flowers in the course of a day's work. But what if a much smaller buzzer bee finds her way inside? She can take the pollen without ever losing any of it by touching a sticky stigma. European honeybees that have been introduced to America have taken up buzzing in this way in Mexico. They're smaller than Mexican bees and they're making a good living as pollen thieves.

Maybe plants can afford to lose nectar, but they can't afford to lose pollen, so pollen larceny could turn out to be serious. Biologists have tested this in South Africa by placing hives of native honeybees among stands of soap aloe (*Aloe maculata*), which is pollinated mainly by birds. They found the honeybees stole pollen without contributing to pollination and another group of native bees were also stealing pollen. After the hives were introduced, seed production declined. Theft harms the victim.

Stingless bees (*Trigona species*) have also been convicted of pollen thievery, as have hoverflies and ants. Thieves tend to remain for longer in the flowers they're robbing than do honest pollinators. They seem to have all the time in the world to collect as much loot as they can carry. And it's not only the anthers that suffer from their pilfering. They'll even take pollen from stigmas, a practice that risks damaging the stigma,

Two hummingbird species pollinate yellow *Jacobinia* (*Justicia aurea*),
of tropical Central America, and defend the nectar, but a third smaller
bird steals nectar by piercing the corolla. Stingless bees and ants also
rob the flower, seriously depleting its store of nectar.

either physically or by chemical contamination, and there are orchid pollinators that have found ways to steal pollinia. Hawk moths pollinate certain plants, but they're also notorious pollen thieves.

Most thieves simply enter the flower, through an unlocked door or open window as it were, steal its pollen, and leave, but a few thieves break their way in, damaging the flower. These are small bees that steal from flowers pollinated by hummingbirds, biting through the corolla to reach the anthers, deep inside. The hummingbirds aren't interested in pollen, of course, but by the time they call for their nectar it may be too late for the flower to dust them with pollen and, with its petals damaged, the flower is likely to wilt and fall faster than it would have done had it remained intact.

Birds and insects aren't the only thieves around. Bats pollinate baobab flowers, but bush babies also visit. They pollinate the flowers to some extent, but they also steal pollen. In Madagascar, where nocturnal lemurs and fruit bats pollinate baobabs, the lemurs may be stealing pollen too.

What makes a victim and can you have degrees of victim? If you're mugged in the street, that's bad luck, but it might make you wonder whether something in your appearance, the way you walk, your manner, somehow identified you as a likely target. That's distressing enough, but what if you were mugged repeatedly on the way home? What would you think then?

I mention the possibility because certain plants seem to be multiple victims. Take yellow jacobinia (*Justicia aurea*), for instance. It grows in Central America and hummingbirds pollinate its flower. So far so good, but there are smaller hummingbirds that can't reach the nectar. These attack through the side, as primary nectar thieves. The holes they make in the corollas allow ants and bees access to what's left of the nectar, so they enter as secondary thieves. But then, to cap it all, small stingless bees crawl in and steal the pollen. It's enough to make the plant want to give up.

Plants aren't entirely helpless, however. Common vetch, elder, peony, peach and passionflower are among more than two thousand species of plants that defeat robbers by diverting them. They have nectaries located on leaves, stems, fruits, and other parts of the plant, well away from the flowers. Ants find these extrafloral nectaries much more accessible than nectaries in their more traditional location, buried at the base of flowers. The robbers take only the nectar, leaving the pollen intact.

Alternatively, you might cover exterior surfaces with hairs or spikes to make them difficult for walking insects to cross. Attach the hairs to poison glands, so would-be thieves receive a large dose of something extremely unpleasant, and the deterrent works even better.

A sticky coat also makes life difficult for insect pedestrians. Their feet keep sticking to it. If stickiness doesn't appeal, what about slipperiness? A layer of wax might do the trick by making a very smooth surface. Then you could make the flowers difficult to reach by arranging them so they hang downward on slender stalks and wave about in the slightest breath of wind.

The most obvious defence is simply to toughen up the regions where invaders are most likely to enter. Many plants that have a pollinating contract with hummingbirds do this, making the calyx around the base of the flower too thick for the birds to tear open or drill through. But the strategy works for other members of the criminal classes as well. Examine the base of the flowers of pinks or campion, for example, and see how thick the tissue is. That's to protect the organs inside against robbers.

Melastomataceae is a family of more than five thousand tropical plants with no common name because those that have wandered outside their native territories have turned out to be invasive weeds, so no one wants them around. But some of them have developed by far the subtlest way of dealing with burglars; they deceive them into becoming pollinators. The plants achieve this by producing two types of stamen. At the centre of their purple flowers there are conspicuous, bright yellow stamens. Those are the ones the simple-minded pollen thieves make for and, indeed, the stamens do bear pollen.

But it's low-grade pollen and cheap for the plant to make. In order to reach the yellow stamens, however, the thieves must cross an outer ring of less prominent purple stamens, and those are the ones bearing the valuable pollen. Thus, as the thieves move from flower to flower seeking their boldly displayed booty and no doubt boasting to themselves that they've outwitted their victim, they pollinate the plants despite themselves. It's rather like fitting a device in your home that automatically hacked into the bank account of any visiting burglar and transferred to your account a sum that was slightly greater than the value of the goods stolen. How clever is that!

We primates can be pollen thieves, too. In 1936, ahead of the opening of the Royal Horticultural Society Show held in Brisbane, Queensland, plant exhibitors went round carefully removing the pollen from their prize blooms. That was to prevent rival breeders from stealing the pollen to develop their own varieties before the exhibitors had had time to market them. Wickedness, you see, knows no bounds.

Teasers
—

Nature's prize confidence tricksters, orchids offer the most delightful of rewards and deliver nothing, while making quite sure that the victims of their con pollinate them. Beyond a doubt, they are the prostitutes of the plant world, and it's win-win for the orchids. Of course, you could criticize their victims for being so stupid as to fall for their wiles over and over again, but where there's dishonesty we shouldn't blame the victim, even if he is a willing sucker.

"Orchids are nature's prize confidence tricksters, offering delightful rewards but delivering nothing."

If you come across a plant hooker there's an odds-on chance it's an orchid. Orchids really go in for this form of deception and they're very good at it. They're also the most diverse of all plants, comprising a family with more than 22,000 species. Why so many? Biologists at the University of Wisconsin have identified three developments in the course of orchid history that led to this huge diversity. The first, starting 60 million years ago, was their invention of pollinia. Once they began packaging their pollen in this way there was a sharp acceleration in the rate at which the orchids were branching into new species. Then, starting 40 million years ago, the orchids colonized high mountains where they were bathed in almost constant rain and mist and at about the same time they learned to live as epiphytes. These events triggered another evolutionary burst, with many more new species. But the greatest boost to their evolution began about 33 million years ago when the Andes, which they'd already colonized, began to rise higher and higher due to tectonic movements. Their invention of pollinia improved pollination, but the second and third developments dispersed the orchids more widely into local groups that were isolated from each other, so they couldn't interbreed. Such reproductive isolation is the condition in which divided populations drift apart genetically and evolve into new species.

As you'd expect with so many species, there's considerable diversity in orchid flowers, but certain features are widespread. The flowers are bilaterally symmetrical, and bisexual in all but a few species, with an outer whorl of three sepals enclosing an inner whorl of three petals. Usually, but not in all species, the sepals and petals are almost indistinguishable, so they're called tepals. The upper middle petal is always bigger than the others and forms a lip called the labellum. As the flower develops the labellum twists around in such a way that it finishes at the bottom, in a position that makes it an ideal platform for insects to land on. The sepals may also be modified and in some species two or all three are fused together. And most orchid flowers have only one viable stamen.

Babyboot orchids (*Lepanthes* species) are a genus of more than eight hundred species found in Central America and parts of South America. They're epiphytes and are pollinated by small flies, up to five millimetres (less than a quarter of an inch) long, known as fungus gnats. These orchids have tiny, complicated but brightly coloured flowers, with a minute labellum resembling a female fungus gnat that has a small attachment called the appendix on the underside. Male fungus gnats are attracted by the flower's scent. When one arrives, approaching from downwind, he first searches for a flower and having found one he walks around it, fanning his wings vigorously, before standing facing the flower, mounting the labellum, and curling his abdomen beneath the labellum and feeling for the appendix, which he grasps with the claspers he uses to hold females for mating. Then he leaves the labellum and turns round to face away from the flower, and it's while making this movement that his abdomen brushes against a pollinium, which sticks to him. The gnat remains in this position usually for just a few minutes, sometimes longer, until he has ejaculated, then he releases his claspers, moves away, and grooms his antennae. After resting he flies away in search of another flower with which to make love. Not perverted but merely stupid, he can't tell the difference between his true love and an admittedly cunning flower. But so far as the orchid is concerned the gnat has served his purpose and the gnat is happy because he doesn't know he's been fooled. The act he performs is called pseudocopulation. Now and again he must meet a genuine female gnat, of course, otherwise there'd be no baby gnats and that wouldn't do at all. The orchids would lose their pollinators.

The bee orchid (*Ophrys apifera*) is probably the most notorious of the cheating orchids. It occurs throughout central and southern Europe, North Africa and the Middle East, and it's also found in Ireland and southern England. Where it does occur it's fairly common. Its sepals are pink, its petals green, and its velvety labellum resembles a female bee or wasp. The plant grows up to about sixty centimetres (two feet) tall and

produces between two and five flowers arranged one above the other on the upright stem. The flower emits a scent like that of a female bee or wasp, so males hurry upwind to find it. Only there's something odd here. If you live in the north, all the honeybees and bumblebees that you see around the flowers will be female workers, so the 'female' orchid has no attraction for them. Indeed, the plant isn't trying to attract them because in the northern part of its range it pollinates itself and prefers it that way. True, insects do visit it and some pseudocopulate with it, but they don't pollinate it. When the orchid's pollinia are mature, they dangle downward until they fall on to the stigma below, and no pollinator is called for.

The bee orchid is mainly a plant of more southerly latitudes, around the Mediterranean, however, and it's there that the deceit pays off. Mediterranean bee orchids really do rely on bees to pollinate them. These are solitary, long-horned bees, the name referring to their very long antennae, and both males and females rummage among the flowers, combining the search for food with the search for partners. And that's how the male gets fooled into picking up a pollinium.

The scent the orchid releases matches exactly the scent of a female of the particular species the orchid has recruited. There are many *Ophrys* species, some with a reddish-brown labellum with green markings, others with a green labellum, and one called the wasp orchid which has a narrower, blotchy labellum ending with a point – the 'sting'. Each orchid has its own bee or wasp pollinator and associated perfume, hence the differences in appearance. In each species, males are seeking females for mating. The orchid doesn't attract females, but by closely imitating a female in scent and appearance, it attracts males, and as he pseudocopulates with what he imagines is the love of his life, or at any rate the love of the moment, he collects a pollinium that he delivers to the stigma of the next bee orchid he visits.

The flower of the bee orchid (*Ophrys fuciflora*) on the right
of this illustration is modified so its labellum closely resembles
a female bee, inviting males to mate.

Tongue orchids, about twenty species of *Cryptostylis*, occur throughout much of southern Asia and in Australia and New Zealand. All of the Australian species rely on a particular ichneumon wasp for pollination. For obvious reasons, if unkindly, the wasp, *Lissopimpla excelsa*, is known as the orchid dupe wasp, and its pseudocopulatory technique is similar to that of the fungus gnats that fall for babyboot orchids.

With bee orchids, both the shape and colour of the flower mimic those of a female bee or wasp and the resemblance is striking. Tongue orchids are slightly different. Their flowers have the right shape, but if you could see one side by side with an orchid dupe wasp you'd notice the colours are different. The flowers are mainly maroon, orange-red, or pink and green, and the wasp is orange and black. The wasp is fooled because both the flower and the wasp itself reflect light predominantly in the ultraviolet (UV) waveband. Insects see well in UV. We don't, but if we did the flower and wasp would look similar to us, too. In addition, there are two small bumps on the flower that stand out prominently in UV, and a female wasp has similar bumps on her wings. The pollinia are bright yellow, and clearly displayed, and ichneumon wasps are strongly attracted to yellow.

There's even an orchid that mimics humans. The blunt-leaved orchid (*Platanthera obtusata*) gives off chemicals that are also found in human body odour. They're not trying to attract humans, of course, but tiger mosquitoes (*Aedes albopictus*). The smell is so faint that humans, even those with a keen sense of smell, can barely detect it. But female tiger mosquitoes, in need of a meal of blood to nourish the eggs developing inside them, can recognize it from afar and they find it irresistible. There's no blood awaiting them, of course, but in their search for the non-existent snack they collect and deliver pollen.

The flower of the tongue orchid (*Cryptostylis arachnites*) has a labellum modified to resemble a female ichneumon wasp.

There is also evidence that cheating increases the efficiency of cross-pollination and that cheating orchids produce higher-quality seeds. Cheating pays off, but we've always suspected that, haven't we? Maybe the honest rewarders hope to win brand loyalty. Who knows?

It works for the orchids, but sexual deception also carries risks. Pseudocopulating males lose sperm, a fact that doesn't concern the flowers in the least. And the flowers are very good at deception. Insects have been observed breaking off copulation with a female to pseudocopulate with a flower and to prefer flowers to genuine females, while some flowers force male insects to ejaculate. All this trickery is fine for the orchid, but it means missed mating opportunities for the insects and over time that could reduce their numbers – which would eventually lead to reduced pollination for the flowers, of course.

When orchids and insects sit for intelligence tests, I wonder who comes out on top?

Fruits without seeds
—

In the end, the purpose of all this trickery and exhibitionism is the production of seeds, and once its seeds are ready to leave, the plant faces a new problem. It needs some way to disperse them. This is important. If the plant just let its seeds fall to the ground, they would be spread fairly thickly around its base. When the young plants started to grow they'd be competing with each other and with their parent for space, water and nutrients. There wouldn't be enough of these resources to go round, the parent would shade its progeny, and, inevitably, most of the seedlings would die. Disperse the seeds, on the other hand, and even though some will fall on stony or otherwise inhospitable ground many more will have a chance to survive than would be the case if they stayed at home. It's the same the whole world over, isn't it? Eventually, no matter how much you love them, you feel an irresistible urge to kick them out. You can hear the birds every spring, bellowing 'Fly, dammit!' as their startled fledglings flounder at the prospect of their first solo.

Orchids produce tiny seeds, like dust, that blow about on the wind, so they don't need any assistance. Neither do the many trees that produce winged seeds, the ones you see spinning as they drift, like little helicopters. But others do need help and so, as I'm sure you'd expect by now, the plants recruit animals. There are seeds that tangle themselves in the fur of animals that brush against them, and burrs that cling to almost any surface. We're included in the recruitment, too, and I don't mean because of the burrs we spend hours picking off our clothes and our pets. We chuck those away.

No, we disperse seeds by collecting the fruits that plants use to bribe us, eating the sweet, fleshy parts, and throwing away the seeds wherever we happen to be, which is usually a long way from the plants that produced them. All fruit-eating animals do this, in some cases swallowing the seeds and then depositing them far away in their plant-nutrient-rich faeces.

It all works perfectly well, but some plants are never satisfied. They want their animal servants to sow the seeds properly as well as transporting them to suitable sites. How do they achieve this? Through trickery, naturally.

There's a South African plant, *Ceratocaryum argenteum*, which stands up to three metres (ten feet) tall and resembles a rush. It lives in an environment that is swept by fire from time to time and its seeds can't survive burning, but they're safe once they're buried below ground, where the fire doesn't penetrate. And, of course, the seeds need to be buried in order to germinate. The seeds resemble nuts and are enclosed in a husk, the finished object being almost perfectly spherical and about 1.5 centimetres (½ inch) across. When they're ripe they fall to the ground. I say 'ripe' deliberately, because these fruits are about the same size and closely resemble the faecal pellets left by local antelopes. What's more, they smell like those pellets. A team of scientists led by Jeremy Midgley of the Universities of Cape Town and KwaZulu Natal sought to discover what animals might eat these seeds. They found that the striped field mouse eats them, but only those that have lost their husks, and they noted that when they lost their husks the seeds also lost their perfume. Then they saw that dung beetles were rolling the seeds along the ground, just as though they were dung balls. The famously industrious beetles, standing on their forelegs and pushing with their back legs, were shifting seeds much bigger than themselves.

To check them out, the researchers collected 195 seeds and left them at 31 different sites. When they returned a day later they found more than one-quarter of the seeds had been taken away and buried. Dung beetles bury dung balls in moist soil and lay their eggs in them, eating some of the material while they're at it. The larvae then feed on the dung. When the scientists dug up seeds the beetles had buried, they found no beetle eggs on or near them and no bite marks on the husks. Clearly, the beetles had discovered their mistake when they tried to tunnel into the 'balls', but that wasn't until after they'd buried them. Great for the plant and in this case you can't accuse the beetles of stupidity. All the same, they received no reward and went ambling on their way, no doubt hoping that the next ball they collected would be made of real dung.

But in the end, smart though they may be, the plants are no match for high-street greengrocers and the plant breeders that develop the stock they sell. Take bananas. Peel a banana and you can eat all of it. It's definitely a fruit, but it's a fruit without seeds. How can that be? The very word 'fruit' implies a structure enclosing seeds. Without seeds how can the plant reproduce?

The fruit of the banana is a berry and in the wild ancestor of our cultivated bananas it is a berry that contains seeds. This illustration shows the edible banana *Musa acuminata*.

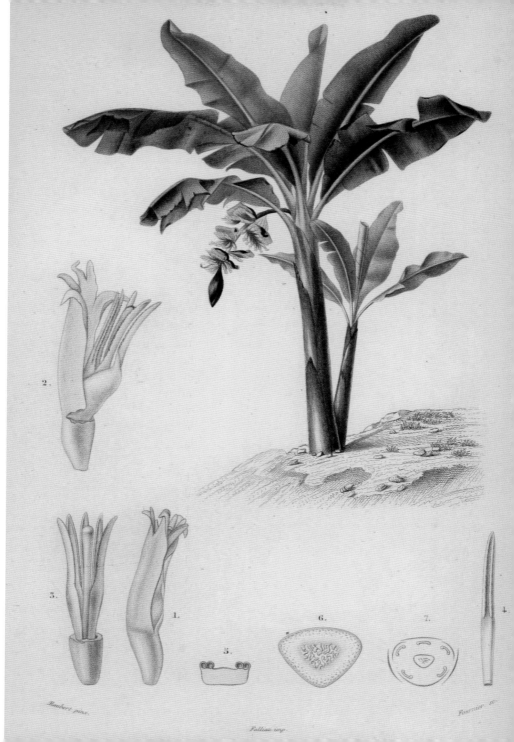

Seedlessness can come about naturally, by mutation, but plant breeders can also make it happen. The fruit of the banana is a berry and wild relatives of the cultivated banana produce berries containing up to about sixty seeds. The cells of some banana plants contain two sets of chromosomes (diploid) while the cells of other species contain four sets (tetraploid). When a diploid plant is crossed with one that's tetraploid the progeny inherits one set of chromosomes from its diploid parent and two sets from its tetraploid parent, so it has three sets (triploid). The triploid condition makes it impossible for the cells to divide the chromosomes evenly to produce sperm and ovules, so it's unable to produce seeds. How does it reproduce? In a sense, it doesn't. Growers propagate it from cuttings. Seedless watermelons are produced in much the same way, but in their case some of the fruits contain just a few seeds, which can be sown to produce more melons. The fact is that seedless fruits are much easier and pleasanter to eat, so since folk have been alerted to the possibility there's been no end to the development of them.

This wild relative of the cultivated banana contains seeds. The fruit we eat today has been cultivated into a seedless variety to make it easier to eat.

Growers have cultivated seedless grapes since the nineteenth century. They're grown from cuttings, and they do produce seeds, but as the fruits mature a genetic abnormality prevents the seeds from developing and they're absorbed into the flesh of the grape. The variety probably originated in the Caucasus.

There are also seedless citrus fruits. Navel oranges are descended from a single mutant tree found on a Brazilian plantation in the nineteenth century. All today's navel oranges are grown from cuttings, so they're all clones of that first tree. Growers produce other seedless citrus fruits by crossing varieties that are genetically incompatible. This means they can't be pollinated, but fruits develop anyway.

Do we win, then? Only to a very limited extent. We gain those fruits we prefer, but at the price of propagating the plants ourselves, which is time-consuming. In a word, we have to work for it.

Meanwhile, back in the wide wild world, the plants go their way as they have always done, caring nothing for us – not a fig, you might say. Each in their season, they open their flowers, release their pollen, produce their fruits and seeds, and life goes on. Our gardens mimic that. And as the Sunday families strolling in the park admire the sexual vigour of the flowerbeds, perhaps they may turn a blind eye to all the desperate deceit, cheating and entrapment that underlies the pretty display. As a visitor to a vast rainforest might remark, 'It's a jungle out there.'

USEFUL INFORMATION

Further Reading

—

Chapter 1

Bell, Adrian D. *Plant Form: An Illustrated Guide to Flowering Plant Morphology.* Expanded and updated edition, Timber Press, Portland, Oregon, 2008.

Sponberg, Simon, Jonathan P. Dyhr, Robert W. Hall and Thomas L. Daniel. 'Luminance-dependent visual processing enables moth flight in low light.' *Science*, pp. 1245–1248, June 12, 2015.

Trewavas, Anthony. *Plant Behaviour & Intelligence.* Oxford University Press, Oxford, 2014.

Chapter 2

Hansen, Dennis M., and Christine B. Müller. 'Invasive ants disrupt gecko pollination and seed dispersal of the endangered plant *Roussea simplex* in Mauritius.' *Biotropica*, 42(2), 202–208. 2009. Abstract online at http://www.jstor.org/stable/20492551?seq=1#page_scan_tab_contents

Kew Gardens. *Roussea simplex.* http://www.kew.org/science-conservation/plants-fungi/roussea-simplex

Olesen, Jens M. and Alfredo Valido. 'Lizards as pollinators and seed dispersers: an island phenomenon.' *Trends in Ecology and Evolution*, 18(4), April 4, 2003. Online at http://podarcis.de/AS/Bibliografie/BIB_1822.pdf

Smithsonian Marine Station at Fort Pierce. *Ipomoea pes-caprae* (Railroad Vine). http://www.sms.si.edu/irlspec/Ipomoea_pesCap.htm

The Evolution of Sexual Reproduction. *The Journal of Evolutionary Philosophy*. http://www.evolutionary-philosophy.net/sex.html

Verduijn, M. H., P. J. Van Dijk and J. M. M. Van Damme, 'The role of tetraploids in the sexual–asexual cycle in dandelions (*Taraxacum*). *Heredity*, 93, 390–398, July 7, 2004. Online at http://www.nature.com/hdy/journal/v93/n4/full/6800515a.html

Chapter 3
'Gall Flowers In Figs.' http://waynesword.palomar.edu/gallfig.htm

Grossenbacher, Dena, Ryan Briscoe Runquist, Emma E. Goldberg and Yaniv Brandvain. 'Geographic range size is predicted by plant mating system.' *Ecology Letters*, vol. 18, no. 7, 706–713, July 2015. Abstract online at http://onlinelibrary.wiley.com/doi/10.1111/ele.12449/abstract

Ramya, K. T., R. Abdul Fiyaz, R. Uma Shaanker and K. N. Ganeshaiah. 'Pollinators for a synconium: How do wasps choose among synconia?' *Current Science*, vol. 101, no. 4, August 2011. Online at http://www.currentscience.ac.in/Volumes/101/04/0520.pdf

Shales, Sarah. 'The pin and thrum of primroses.' https://plantscientist.wordpress.com/2013/04/27/organism-of-the-week-primrose-primula-vulgaris/

Totland, Ørjan and Matteo Sottocornola. 'Pollen limitation of reproductive success in two sympatric alpine willows (Salicaceae) with contrasting pollination strategies.' *American Journal of Botany*, 88(6): 1011–1015, 2011. Online at http://www.amjbot.org/content/88/6/1011.full.pdf

Yasuhiro Sato, Koh-Ichi Takakura, Sachiko Nishida and Takayoshi Nishida. 'Dominant occurrence of cleistogamous flowers of *Lamium amplexicaule* in relation to the nearby presence of an alien congener *L. purpureum* (Lamiaceae)'. ISRN Ecology, vol. 2013, article ID 476862. Online at http://www.hindawi.com/journals/isrn/2013/476862/

Chapter 4
Wiens, Frank, Annette Zitzmann, Marc-André Lachance, Michel Yegles, Fritz Pragst, Friedrich M. Wurst, Dietrich von Holst, Saw Leng Guan and Rainer Spanagel. 'Chronic intake of fermented floral nectar by wild treeshrews.' PNAS, vol. 105, no. 30, July 29, 2008. Online at http://www.pnas.org/content/105/30/10426.long

Chapter 5
Botanical Society of America. BSA Parasitic Plant Pages: *Hydnora africana.* http://botany.org/Parasitic_Plants/Hydnora_africana.php

Celebrezze, Thomas Martin. 'Effects of European honeybees (*Apis mellifera*) on the pollination ecology of bird- and insect-adapted Australian plants.' Doctor of Philosophy thesis, University of Wollongong, 2002. Online at http://ro.uow.edu.au/theses/1046/

Getz, Wayne M. and Katherine B. Smith. 'Olfactory sensitivity and discrimination of mixtures in the honeybee *Apis mellifera*.' *Journal of Comparative Physiology A*, vol. 160, pp. 239–245, 1987. Online at http://nature.berkeley.edu/getzlab/Reprints/Getz%26SmithJCompPhys87.pdf

Kew Gardens. *Amorphophallus titanium* (titan arum). http://www.kew.org/science-conservation/plants-fungi/amorphophallus-titanum-titan-arum

Kew Gardens. *Rafflesia arnoldii* (corpse flower). http://www.kew.org/science-conservation/plants-fungi/rafflesia-arnoldii-corpse-flower

Milius, Susan. 'Warm-blooded plants? OK, there's no blood, but they do make their own heat.' *Science News Online*. http://www.phschool.com/science/science_news/articles/warm_blooded_plants.html

Whelan, Robert J., David J. Ayre and Fiona M. Beynon. 'The birds and the bees: pollinator behaviour and variation in the mating system of the rare shrub *Grevillea macleayana*.' *Annals of Botany*, 103(9), 1395–1401. June 2009. Online at http://www.ncbi.nlm.nih.gov/pmc/articles/PMC2701754/

Chapter 6

Carl Linnaeus (1707–1778). http://www.ucmp.berkeley.edu/history/linnaeus.html

Chapter 7

Seymour, Roger S. and Philip G. D. Matthews, 'The role of thermogenesis in the pollination biology of the Amazon waterlily *Victoria amazonica*.' Annals of Botany, vol. 98(6), December 2006. Online at http://www.ncbi.nlm.nih.gov/pmc/articles/PMC2803590/

Chapter 8

Blanco, Mario A., and Gabriel Barboza. 'Pseudocopulatory pollination in *Lepanthes* (Orchidaceae: Pleurothallidinae) by fungus gnats.' *Annals of Botany*, vol. 95, pp. 763–772, 2005. Online at http://aob.oxfordjournals.org/content/95/5/763.full.pdf

Coyne, Jerry. 'A new and bizarre form of mimicry: plant seeds mimic shape and smell of animal feces to facilitate dispersal by dung beetles.' *Why Evolution is True*. Online at whyevolutionistrue.wordpress.com/2015/10/07/a-new-and-bizarre-form-of-mimicry-plant-seeds-mimic-shape-and-smell-of-animal-feces-to-facilitate-dispersal-by-dung-beetles/

Gasket, A. C., C. G. Winnick and M. E. Herberstein. 'Orchid Sexual Deceit Provokes Ejaculation.' *The American Naturalist*, vol. 171, No. 6., June 2008. Online at https://www.amherst.edu/media/view/120414/original/Gaskettv 2008.pdf

Gasket, A. C., and M. E. Herberstein. 'Colour mimicry and sexual deception by Tongue orchids (Cryptostylis).' *Naturwissenschaften*, vol. 97, 97–102, 2010. Online at http://www.researchgate.net/publication/26864847_Colour_mimicry_and_sexual_deception_by_Tongue_orchids_(Cryptostylis)

Jersáková, Jana, Steven D. Johnson and Pavel Kindlmann. 'Mechanism and evolution of deceptive pollination in orchids.' *Biological Reviews*, vol. 81, pp. 219–235. Cambridge Philosophical Society, 2006. Online at web.natur.cuni.cz/uzp/data/2006_deception.pdf

Maruyama, Pietro Kiyoshi, Jeferson Vizentin-Bugoni, Bo Dalsgaard, Ivan Sazima and Marlies Sazima. 'Nectar robbery by a hermit hummingbird: association to floral phenotype and its influence on flowers and network structure.' *Oecologia*, DOI 10.1007/s00442-0125-3275-9. Published online 6 March 2015. http://www.researchgate.net/profile/Jeferson_Vizentin-Bugoni/publication/273149388_Nectar_robbery_by_a_hermit_hummingbird_association_to_floral_phenotype_and_its_influence_on_flowers_and_network_structure/links/54ff05420cf2eaf210b48db9.pdf

Murphy, Christina M. and Michael D. Breed. 'Nectar and Resin Robbing in Stingless Bees.' *American Entomologist*, Spring 2008. Online at http://www.entsoc.org/PDF/Pubs/Periodicals/AE/AE-2008/Spring/Breed.pdf

Robertson, Don. *Bird Families of the World: Sunbirds and Spiderhunters*, Nectariniidae. http://creagrus.home.montereybay.com/sunbirds.html

Index

—

Picture acknowledgements

—

Illustrations on pages 24, 55, 79, 112, 118, 143, 153, 222 © Sandra Pond.

Front cover B. Hoola van Nooten, *Fleurs, fruits et feuillages choisis de l'Ile de Java*, 1880; page 2 R.J. Thornton, *New illustration of the sexual system of Carolus von Linnaeus and the temple of Flora, or garden of nature*, 1807; page 15 Christiaan Sepp, *Flora Batava*, Vol. 1 (The Hague, 1880); page 18 Otto Wilhelm Thomé, *Flora von Deutschland Österreich und der Schweiz* (Gera, Germany, 1885); page 22 Otto Wilhelm Thomé, *Flora von Deutschland, Österreich und der Schweiz*, (Gera, Germany, 1885); page 27 Franz Eugen Köhler, *Köhlers Medizinal-Pflanzen*, 1887; page 28 Christiaan Sepp, in Janus (Jan) Kops, *Flora Batava of Beschrijving van Nederlandsche Gewassen*, vol. 2, 1807; page 31 Franz Eugen Köhler, *Köhlers Medizinal-Pflanzen*, 1887; Page 36 Didier Descouens/Creative Commons; page 39 Franz Eugen Köhler, *Köhlers Medizinal-Pflanzen*, 1887; page 42 Franz Eugen Köhler, *Köhlers Medizinal-Pflanzen*, 1887; page 46 Javier Rubilar/Creative Commons; page 65 Jeevan Jose, Kerala, India/Creative Commons; page 49 A. van der Laan, in N. L. Burman, *Flora Indica*, 1768; page 53 W. H. Fitch, *Curtis's Botanical Magazine, vol 74*, 1848; page 61 John Curtis, *British Entomology, vol 5*, 1840s; page 67 Gottorfer Codex, 1649-1659; page 72 L. van Houtte, *Flore des serres et des jardins de l'Europe*, 1845; page 73 J. G. Keulemans in Alfred Grandidier *Histoire physique, naturelle et politique de Madagascar* (1875-1897); page 77 F. Losch, *Kräuterbuch, unsere Heilpflanzen in Wort und Bild, Zweite Auflage*, t. 70, fig. 1, 1905; page 85 Franz Eugen Köhler, *Köhlers Medizinal-Pflanzen*, 1887; page 95 F. W. van Eeden, in Janus (Jan) Kops, *Flora Batava of Beschrijving van Nederlandsche Gewassen*, 1885; page 100 J. Barrellier, J., *Plantae per Galliam, Hispaniam et*

Italiam observatae, t. 261-264, fig. 264, 1714; page 106 Otto Wilhelm Thomé *Flora von Deutschland, Österreich und der Schweiz* (Gera, Germany, 1885); page 117 O.W. *Thomé, Flora von Deutschland Österreich und der Schweiz*, Tafeln, vol. 1: t. 50 (Gera, Germany, 1885), page 122 Franz Eugen Köhler, *Köhlers Medizinal-Pflanzen*, vol 3, t 34, 1890; page 127 W. H. Fitch, in *Curtis's Botanical Magazine*, vol. 77, 1851; page 134 Joseph Wolf, *Proceedings of the Zoological Society of London*, Mamm pl. 2, 1848; page 135 Joseph Smit in R. Lydekker, "*On two lorises*". *Proceedings of the Zoological Society*. Volume II. Plate XXIII, 1904; page 137 W. H. Harvey, *Thesaurus capensis, or illustrations of South African flora*, vol. 1: t. 32, 1859; page 142 Otto Wilhelm Thomé, *Flora von Deutschland, Österreich und der Schweiz* (Gera, Germany, 1885); page 157 Charles Darwin, *On the Various Contrivances by which British and Foreign Orchis are Fertilised by Insects, and on the Good Effects of Intercrossing* (John Murray, London, 1862); page 158 Bob Peterson/Creative Commons; page 162 Franz Eugen Köhler, *Köhlers Medizinal-Pflanzen*, vol 2, t 175, 1890; page 164 Pierre-Joseph Redouté, *Les Roses*, Paris 1817–24, p. 290; page 166 Franz Eugen Köhler, *Köhlers Medizinal-Pflanzen*, 1887; page 167 Jacob Rus/Creative Commons; page 169 Matilda Smith in *Curtis's Botanical Magazine*, vol. 117, pl. 7153, 1891; page 170 Franz Bauer, *Transactions of the Linnean Society of London*, vol. 13, 1822; page 175 A. Bertrand, *Les trochilidées* (Paris 1832?); page 177 S.T. Edwards *Botanical Magazine*, vol. 8, t. 260, 1794; page 178 Matilda Smith in *Curtis's Botanical Magazine*, vol. 47, ser. 3, vol. 47: t. 7209, 1891; page 179 *Magasin de Zoologie: d'anatomie comparée et de paléontologie*, 1832; page 181 J.W. Weinmann, *Phytanthoza iconographia*, vol. 3: t. 600, fig. a, 1742; page 186 Widdell sc in *Curtis's Botanical Magazine*, vol. 44, pl. 1932, 1817; page 189 *Botanical Magazine*, vol. 1: t. 2,

1787; page 190 Otto Wilhelm Thomé, *Flora von Deutschland, Österreich und der Schweiz* (Gera, Germany, 1885); page 196 Jacob Sturm, in Johann Georg Sturm, *Deutschlands Flora in Abbildungen* 1796; page 199 L. van Houtte, *Flore des serres et des jardin de l'Europe*, vol. 8: t. 755, 1853; page 203 Joseph Smit in *The Ibis*, ser. 3, vol. 5, 1875; page 208 W.H. Fitch *Curtis's Botanical Magazine*, vol. 75, ser. 3, vol. 5, t. 4444, 1849; page 214 Otto Wilhelm Thomé, *Flora von Deutschland, Österreich und der Schweiz* (Gera, Germany, 1885); page 217 Walter Hood Fitch, *Curtis's Botanical Magazine*, vol. 89, 1863; page 221 C. V. D. d'Orbigny, *Dictionnaire universel d'histoire naturelle*, vol. 3, 1841–9.

All images in the book are in the public domain unless otherwise noted. Every effort has been made to credit the copyright holders. The author and publisher would be glad to amend in future editions any errors or omissions brought to their attention.

About the Author

—

Michael Allaby has been writing all his life – it all began with a detective story, which he wrote aged seven in indelible pencil to give it permanence. In 1971, he published his first book about the birth of the environmental movement and he's been a full-time writer ever since. Popular science is his speciality and he is editor of several dictionaries for Oxford University Press and author of a dictionary of science for gardeners and a gardener's guide to weather for Timber Press. Michael takes pleasure in sharing the richness of the world around him, exploring the way things work and teasing out answers to his own questions. He still enjoys telling stories and although for the most part he's moved on from writing crime, enjoyed this foray into the dark underbelly of the plant world.